A GUIDE TO KYOGEN

A Guide to Kyogen

by Don Kenny

Hinoki Shoten

Published by Hinoki Shoten
2–1, Kanda Ogawa-cho, Chiyoda-ku, Tokyo

Printed by Azuma Printing Co., Tokyo :

First edition, 1968

Printed in Japan

CONTENTS

Introduction   7

Author's Preface   11

Synopscs   15

INTRODUCTION

Noh is usually about gods and spirits, it is idealistic drama which peers deeply into the mysteries of the spirit; Kyōgen is always about human beings and even its gods are obviously mortal. It has no use for that ideal face, the mask; it does not need music because there is no mystery to suggest; nor is it slow, stately, or poetic: its language is vernacular and its tempo is faster than life. Kyōgen is satyrplay, anti-masque; it is Pyramis and Thisbe to Noh's Theseus and Hippolyta. Taking place in the kitchen, near the warm hearth, leaving the cold if stately hall to the deities, it is resolutely and resoundly human.

It was human frailty which created Kyōgen since it was originally intended to obviate the sublime and unavoidable boredom of the Noh. Though its ancestry is plebeian, though that of the Noh is aristocratic, an alliance was arranged between the two houses and the marriage still holds. Even now a Kyōgen is usually sandwiched between two Noh plays, or even between halves of a single drama; even now the marriage shows what all successful marriages must—a dazzling contrast.

The Noh concludes, the last wraith slides away; the Kyōgen begins, suddenly the carpenters appear. They open their mouths and we fall from the clouds and land with a bump, just as does one of the gods in their plays. Moved by the Noh, transfigured, a better and ideal world opening before us, our eyes wet with its beauty, we—the audience—become a part of the great and single comic plot when, bounced back into reality by the Kyōgen, we discover that we too have two hands and a nose like everyone else, and that those funny people in front of us are ourselves. And we are hilarious because one of the astonishing things about Kyōgen is that it is so very funny—not to read, perhaps, but then the text of a Labiche farce or a Keaton film, or even a Molière play, is not that funny to read. Comedy, unlike tragedy, lies in the doing.

The Kyōgen doings are based on a slender repertoire of situations. A lord has a stupid servant (always called Tarō Kaja, just as Charlot is always Charlot, Buster is always Buster) who cannot tell a fan from an umbrella, or who inadvertently gives away to his mistress his master's philanderings, or who drinks up all the *saké* and fills up the bottles with hot water and then tries to talk the master into thinking he is getting drunk. Tarō is joined by a large cast of comic characters, each as distinctive as himself, just as sublimely stupid, as gloriously sly, as eternally innocent. For it is our foibles which Kyōgen celebrates, just as the Noh illuminates our aspirations. Comic situations are as limited as tragic and it is their scarcity which links the great and presumably opposed houses of tears and laughter, which enables great minds to flap the plots over like flapjacks and which shows us that Hamlet and Don Quixote are really first cousins. The audience, after all, has only two minds of which to be and the Kyōgen says: Come on, be yourselves.

Not, then, for the Kyōgen actor the brocades of Noh, those great, living landscapes for the back. Instead, he wears kitchen colors—brown, grey, all in checks and squares and diamonds. Clean, neat, starched and common, he is nonetheless ready to run and fall down. And when he races off at

8

the end of the play, it is not, one feels, to that mirrored room of the Noh actor, chamber for meditation, for communion with the mysterious self. No, it is straight for the kitchen and the warm fire and a cup of hot *saké* taken with smacking lips.

He is a real professional, the Kyōgen actor. He delivers fast, is always on his feet, a real stand-up comic. He bubbles over, he aspirates, he is very funny. Yet—and here he shares with the greatest of comedians—he is never vulgar. Zeami, the man who invented Japanese dramaturgy, speaks loud and clear from the depths of the fourteenth century when he says that Kyōgen should "kindle the mind to laughter," but that "neither in speech nor in gesture should there be anything low. The jokes and repartee . . . . however funny they may be, should not introduce the vulgar."

Hence, perhaps, the warmth, the charm. In Kyōgen one senses that the actor, knowing perfectly well that he is impersonating a comic, also feels that both breeding and goodwill insist that he hide this fact. He is never a wise-guy. He is observing what Zeami himself was probably only observing when he laid down the law that there should be "a tinge of unreality in reality," a "refinement and concentration of all conflicting qualities into one dominant note." This note seems to sound in the ears of only the greatest of comedians: you, a human, must impersonate a human.

And the Kyōgen is (if you can put it this way) sublimely human. It celebrates foibles in the way that melodrama celebrates goodness, and that tragedy celebrates devotion. Mistakes, error, sloth, and all of the appetites—these are the stuff of which Kyōgen is made. The mirror that it holds up is not the mirror of Noh, the self alone, communing, but a minutely detailed picture of the world as it is, crowded and crawling, like a street-scene seen through the wrong end of a telescope,

9

a world we know quite well but now find rendered hilariously understandable.

It is half the world, and it knows it. It is one pole of human aspiration, just as Noh is the other. The resulting stress, even strain, is what makes the combination so supremely right. The way we would want to be, the way of aspiration, this is Noh. The way we are, the way to acceptance, this is Kyōgen. And both roads lead to wisdom.

The Kyōgen actor with his air of faint amusement, his just-you-wait-and-see mien, the savoring pucker of a loving artist controlling his comic role—this is a look which says: I know that I am human, only human, with all of our foibles, but this I can accept, just as I can accept the change of seasons, the coming of wrinkles, grey hair and an aching back. This is how things are—my world of Kyōgen is your world as well.

Donald Richie
Tokyo, 1968

10

AUTHOR'S PREFACE

Mr. Richie has so adeptly grasped the essence of Kyōgen in the introduction he so kindly wrote for this book that I will confine my remarks to a few technical points.

Kyōgen is the comedy vignette form which developed alongside of and in conjunction with the Noh Drama. Both of these forms of drama were perfected and flourished during the Muromachi Period (1380–1466). While Noh and Kyōgen are performed on the same stage and there is a part for a Kyōgen actor in almost every Noh play, they are two separate forms. The training of the actors is different and no professional actor performs both forms. Kyōgen dialogue is a somewhat stylized form of the common spoken language of the Muromachi Period while that of Noh is highly literary in style.

This book is designed as a basic guide for the viewer of a Kyōgen performance, therefore it consists of the plots of all the plays in the present repertoire (257 plays), their titles and dramatis personae.

There are two schools of Kyōgen in existence at the present time, the Izumi (和泉) School and the Ōkura (大蔵) School. The Izumi School is made up of the Nomura and Miyake families, and the Ōkura includes the Ōkura, Zenchiku, Yamamoto, and Shigeyama families. There was previously another school called Sagi but it ceased to exist some time during the Meiji Period. The main differences between the two schools lie in a slight difference in the overall style of the language used, that of the Ōkura School being somewhat older; also the use of the voice is somewhat different with the Izumi using a deeper more resonant tone; and the most obvious difference being those cases where the story line is not quite the same. The present repertoire of the Izumi School includes 254 plays while the Ōkura School has 180. There are 71 plays in the Izumi repertoire which are not in the Ōkura, but only 3 in the Ōkura repertoire which are not in the Izumi. This leaves 177 plays which are common to both schools with only slight differences in plot or dialogue.

In this book you will find the letters I and/or O to the right of the title of each play. The letter I stands for Izumi and O for Ōkura, thus those with both I and O are common to both schools, those with only an I only appear in the Izumi repertoire and those with only an O only in the Ōkura repertoire.

The characters in the play are referred to as *shite* meaning "protagonist" and *ado* meaning "antagonist," plus other *ado* (of which there are sometimes many) often referred to as **3rd ado** which are the supporting characters, and *tachishū* which is always a group of walk-on or fill-in type parts.

The Most common characters are quite easy to differentiate between by their stylized costumes. The ubiquitous Tarō Kaja, the eternal servant, is always dressed in a brightly colored checked kimono over which is a stiff vest-like *kataginu* and an ankle-length broad trouser-like *hakama*. The Master wears a *kimono* with soberly colored broad horizontal stripes and a long *hakama* plus the stiff vest-like *kataginu*. A Woman wears a *kimono* with a large flower pattern and a long broad band of white cloth called a *binan bōshi* which is wrapped around the head and hangs all the way down to the waist on both sides. Other characters are even more easily recognized because of their representational costumes and paraphernalia.

The word Kyōgen is often misinterpreted as "farcical interludes" or directly translated as "crazy words," both of which I highly object to. The character 狂 pronounced *kyo* in this case is also the character for the verb *kuruu* which commonly means "to go crazy" but also means "to concentrate on" or "to become completely absorbed in." *Gen* 言 is the character for *iu* which means "to speak" or "to say." The two characters together then mean something like "completely absorbed in speaking."

Kyogen admittedly has many of the characteristics of farce and slapstick which are especially evident in plays like *Bō Shibari* and *Busu*, but there are also those like *Su Hajikami* which enter the realm of high comedy with their clever play on words; those full of pathos and melodramatic aspects such as *Tsurigitsune*, *Kawakami*, and *Mi Kazuki*; those with a twisted sense of humor which almost puts them in the realm of "black comedy" such as *Akutagawa*, *Tsukimi Zatō*, and *Saru Zatō*; and even some which reach great heights of poetry such as *Yūzen*, *Tsūen*, and *Rakuami*. Kyōgen partakes of all the aspects of comedy in the broadest sense of the word. Therefore, if there must be an English name or term attached to this art, I prefer "comedy vignettes."

The following collections of Kyōgen scripts were used for reference in the compilation and writing of this book; *Izumiryū Kyōgen Taisei* compiled by Yamawaki Izumi published by *Wanya* 1917 (和泉流狂言大成, 山脇和泉, わんや), *Kyōgen Sanbyakubanshū* compiled by Nonomura Kaizō and Andō Tsunejirō published by Tomiyama 1938 (狂言三百番集, 野々村戒三 安藤常次郎 富山), *Kyōgen Zenshū* compiled by Tsuruta Kyūsaku published by *Kokumin Bunko Kankōkai* 1910 (狂言全集,鶴田久作,国民文庫刊行会), *Kyōgenhen* compiled by Saitō Kōson published by Yōkyoku Bunko Kai 1928 (狂言篇斎藤香村, 謡曲文庫会) for the Izumi School;

and *Kyōgenshū* compiled by Koyama Hiroshi published by Iwanami 1960 (狂言集, 小山弘志, 岩波), *Noh Kyōgen* compiled by Sasano Ken published by Iwanami 1943 (能狂言, 笹野堅, 岩波), and *Kohon Noh Kyōgenshū* compiled by Sasano Ken published by Iwanami 1943 (古本能狂言集, 笹野堅, 岩波) for the Ōkura School. Also *Kyōgen Jiten* by Furukawa Hisashi published by Tōkyōdō 1963 (狂言辞典, 古川久, 東京堂) was used for general reference.

I wish to express heart-felt thanks first to Mr. Donald Richie who has given me a great deal of advice and encouragement from the beginning, read my original manuscript, and wrote the introduction; next to Mr. Mansaku Nomura, one of the best professional Kyōgen actors and my teacher of Kyōgen as a performing art; to Mr. Yōji Aoi, my secretary and general helper in all matters pertaining to the Japanese language; and to Miss Audie Bock and Miss Suzie Trumbull who so kindly took time to help me read proofs. Also thanks to all those who have given encouragement and expressed interest in this book and the art of Kyōgen.

I hope this book will help the reader gain a deeper understanding and a fuller enjoyment of the most delightful of the lively arts—Kyōgen.

Don Kenny
Tokyo, July '68

SYNOPSES

AKUBŌ 悪坊 (Akubō mends His Ways)

I O
和大

Shite   DRUNKARD (AKUBŌ)
Ado   PRIEST
Koado   MASTER OF TEA SHOP

A Priest on his way home runs into a Drunkard named Akubō. Akubō insists on their travelling together, and along the road he teases and frightens the Priest with his halberd. They come to a tea shop and Akubō insists that they stop and rest because he knows the Master of the tea shop well.

Akubō orders the Priest to massage and pound his hip while he rests. Akubō goes to sleep, and the Master tells the Priest that this Akubō is famous for being a drunkard and for his cruel treatment of those he meets when he is drunk. The Priest decides to leave before Akubō wakens. In return for Akubō's cruel teasing, the Priest takes Akubō's clothes and halberd and leaves his own priest's robes and umbrella.

Akubō wakes up later to find himself with the priest's robes and umbrella. He says the Priest must have been Buddha or Daruma in disguise, and decides to mend his ways and become a monk. He goes off singing to himself, lamenting his fate.

AKAGARI 輝 (Chapped Feet)　　I O
　　　　　　　　　　　　　　　　　　和 大

Shite　　　TARŌ KAJA
Ado　　　MASTER

The Master orders Tarō Kaja to accompany him to a party. On the way, they are discussing the great number of parties recently, and that the Master should give one himself, when they come to a river. The Master orders Tarō Kaja to carry him across, but he refuses saying his feet are terribly chapped, and if they get wet it is unbearably painful. The Master says he will carry Tarō Kaja across, but Tarō Kaja says he can't put his Master to so much trouble. The Master reminds him there is no other way for them to cross the river, so if Tarō Kaja will recite a poem, he can imagine he is carrying a poem instead of Tarō Kaja. The poem is recited. Tarō Kaja gets on his Master's back, and they start across the river. Halfway across the Master demands another poem, after which he gets tired of carrying Tarō Kaja, dumps him in the river, and continues on his way. Tarō Kaja, in the attempt to keep his chapped feet dry, gets thoroughly soaked. He goes off sneezing and grumbling about his sad fate.

18

AKUTAGAWA 芥川
(The Crippled Leg and the Deformed Hand)

I O

和 大

Shite	WORSHIPPER I (MAN WITH A DEFORMED HAND)
Ado	WORSHIPPER II (CRIPPLE)

A Cripple on his way to a temple in Ikuta gets tired and stops to rest along the way. A Man with a deformed hand comes along on his way to the same temple. They decide to travel together. The Cripple insists that the other Man walk ahead because he doesn't want his crippled leg found out.

They come to a river called Akutagawa, and the Man with the deformed hand crosses quickly and easily. The Cripple crosses very slowly and uncertainly, slipping on rocks, etc. The other Man sees that he is a cripple, and makes up the first line of a poem making fun of his handicap. After they have crossed and are washing their hands, the Cripple notices that the other Man never shows his right hand, thus he assumes that it is deformed, so he adds the second line of the previous poem in which he makes fun of the other's deformed hand. The Man objects that his hand is not deformed and proves it by showing his left hand through both sleeves. The Cripple insists that he show his hands once more and this time catches hold of the left hand when it is shown through the left sleeve, thus forcing the Man to show his deformed hand.

The Cripple cries gleefully, "It's deformed! It's deformed!" The Man retorts, "It is not deformed, it is misshapen!" This sends the Cripple into gales of laughter, and the Man with the deformed hand chases him off in an insulted rage.

In the Okura script, the deformed hand is discovered by the Cripple when they are praying together at the temple. The rest is the same as the Izumi script.

AKUTARŌ 悪太郎 (Akutarō Reforms)　　I　O

和　大

Shite　　DRUNKARD (AKUTARŌ)
Ado　　　UNCLE
Koado　　PRIEST

Akutarō is on his way to his Uncle's house, because he has heard that his Uncle has been gossiping about his drinking habits behind his back. He is so angry about it that he has his halberd along to reinforce what he has to say.

By the time Akutarō reaches his Uncle's house he has worked himself into a real temper. Akutarō says he came to show the Uncle the new halberd he has made and sticks it right under his nose. The Uncle is frightened out of his wits. Akutarō demands *saké* and proceeds to criticize everything, even the way his Uncle pours the *saké*.

Akutarō continues to threaten and tease his Uncle till he has gotten all the *saké* he wants and is quite drunk. He starts on his way home, thoroughly satisfied because of his discovery that he can get all the *saké* he wants out of his stingy Uncle by threatening him with the halberd.

On his way home he is so drunk that he mistakes a statue for a man and decides he had better rest for a while. He lies down in the middle of the road and is immediately sound asleep.

The Uncle comes out to see if Akutarō has gotten safely home since he was so drunk and finds him asleep in the middle of the road.

The Uncle decides to pay Akutarō back for his meanness. He exchanges Akutarō's clothes for priests's robes and shaves Akutarō's head and beard, then announces, as though he was a messenger from Buddha himself, that Akutarō must spend the rest of his life praying for forgiveness for his sins, as a priest, and that his name will henceforth be Namu Amida Butsu (actually a Buddhist prayer).

Akutarō wakes up later, finds himself transformed and remembers the voice of the "messenger" as though it had been a dream. A Priest comes by, reciting the Buddhist chant, which includes Namu Amida Butsu. Akutarō answers since he believes it to be his name. The Priest ignores him at first, but finally asks why he is answering as though this were his name. Akutarō tells him the whole story, the Priest tells him the real meaning of the word, and they go off singing a prayer together.

In the Ōkura script, Akutarō has just left a friend's house where he has been drinking, but is not yet satisfied, so he decides to go visit his Uncle who had sent someone saying he wanted to see Akutarō a few days earlier. The Uncle makes Akutarō swear to quit drinking. Akutarō swears he will quit the next day and talks his Uncle into giving him a drink in celebration of this decision. He talks his Uncle into giving him more and more till he finally leaves for home quite drunk. The rest is the same as the Izumi script.

ASAHINA 朝比奈 (Asahina, the Warrior) I O
和 大

Shite   ASAHINA
Ado   EMMA, KING OF HELL

Emma, the King of Hell, has come upon hard days as a result of all the religions which help sinners get to heaven. Things have gotten so bad that he himself has finally come out to the Crossing of the Six Roads to catch sinners and chase them to Hell.

Asahina, the famous warrior, appears and Emma, not recognizing him, tries with all his might to catch Asahina, but his magic powers seem to have no effect. Emma asks why he is so strong. Asahina introduces himself, and shows Emma his seven fearful weapons which are still covered with blood. Emma says if he is the real Asahina, he should know about the Wada Battle. Asahina says he does and proves it by giving a moving account of it in a chanted narrative (*katari*). Asahina then forces Emma to carry his weapons and guide him to heaven.

22

ASŌ 麻生 (Asō has His Hair Fixed)

Shite	DAIMYŌ FROM SHINANO (ASŌ)
Ado	TŌROKU
Koado	GEROKU
Koado	EBOSHI SELLER

A Daimyō from Shinano named Asō calls his servants Tōroku and Geroku and informs them that he has finished his business in the capital and that they will all go home today. Since they haven't been home for a long time, they are very happy. Tōroku suggests that since it has been a long time, the Daimyō should dress in the best ceremonial style for his return trip. The Daimyō agrees, but says he has not made such preparations. Tōroku and Geroku reply that they have made the necessary preparations, that the proper clothes are ready and that the *eboshi* (a ceremonial lacquered hat) has been ordered. The Daimyō says the hair style is very difficult to

do and Tōroku replys that he has learned how to do it. The Daimyō, very happy at the efficiency of his servants, sends Geroku after the hat and orders Tōroku to fix his hair. The hair takes a long time during which the Daimyō asks about various things, such as the pattern and color of the new clothes, etc. Geroku has still not returned when Tōroku has finished fixing the Daimyo's hair, so he goes out in search of him.

Geroku has received the hat on a stick because the lacquer was not yet dry. On the way home he loses his way. Tōroku runs into him and scolds him for forgetting the way to his own master's house. They enter a house and find it is the wrong one. Thus it turns out that Tōroku has also forgotten which house is their master's. This time Geroku does the scolding. They decide to put their problem in a song and in this way search for their master's house. The Daimyō hears them and rewards them with rice cakes for their cleverness.

AWASEGAKI 合柿 (Hybrid Persimmons)   I   O
和 大

Shite PERSIMMON SELLER
Ado HEAD WORSHIPPER
Tachishū NINE WORSHIPPERS

It is festival time, and a Persimmon Seller is bragging that his persimmons are hybrids, that is they include the best qualities of all the good persimmons in the world.

A group of Worshippers comes by, look at the persimmons and claim that they look sour. The Seller objects that they are the sweetest in the world, and offers them one as a free sample. They taste it and it is very sour. The Seller says that anyway

24

the rest are sweet. They force him to taste one himself. It is sour, but he pretends it is sweet. They insist that he whistle to prove what he says. He tries but cannot whistle, so makes several excuses. They only laugh at him and start on their way. He indignantly calls them back and demands payment for the one they ate. When they refuse, he challenges them to a fight. They throw him down, beat and kick him, scatter his persimmons, and go on their way. He picks up himself and his persimmons, and sings his way home sadly and humbly.

In the Ōkura script, a group of Men are on their way to Uji to buy persimmons when they meet the Persimmon Seller on the road. The rest is the same as the Izumi script.

AWATAGUCHI 粟田口   I O
(A Man Poses as a Sword) 和 大

Shite	DAIMYŌ
Ado	TARŌ KAJA
Koado	SHYSTER

A Daimyō sends his servant to the capital to buy an Awataguchi (a famous make of sword). The servant, Tarō Kaja, reaches the capital, and realizing that he doesn't know what an Awataguchi is and since he forgot to ask the Daimyō, he begins shouting that he wants to buy an Awataguchi. A Shyster appears and says that he is an Awataguchi. He explains that Awataguchi is the family name of a famous group of people living in the east part of the capital. He sells himself to Tarō Kaja and they proceed to the Daimyō's house.

The Daimyō doesn't know for sure what an Awataguchi is, but says he doesn't think it is a person and that he has a

document which tells how to recognize a good Awataguchi.
The Shyster agrees to be put to the test of the instructions.
The first test is that there are two kinds, Tōrin and Tōma.
The Shyster says that his name is Tōma. Next that the *habaki*
is black. (*Habaki* means the piece of iron which holds a sword
and its handle together, as well as meaning the black leggings
worn for travel in those days). The Shyster points out that his
leggings are not only black but very dirty. The next test is
that a good Awataguchi has a *mei* (*mei* means "name" and also
"niece"). The Shyster answers that he has an older sister and a
younger sister and each of them has one daughter apiece so
that he has not one but two nieces. The instructions say that
an Awataguchi with two *mei* is of especially fine quality. The
last test is that the *mi* is old (*mi* means "body." In the case of a
sword it means "blade." *Furui*, the word for "old," at that time
also meant "dirty"). The Shyster answers that he hasn't bathed
since he was born so that he is quite dirty.

The Daimyō, confident that he has obtained the best possible
Awataguchi, decides to let Tarō Kaja rest, and takes his new
possession to show it off to his friends. The Daimyō is in such
high spirits that on the way he entrusts the new servant with
both his sword and his dagger. At this point the Shyster
decides it's best for him to disappear while the disappearing
is good, and takes off with the Daimyō's sword and dagger.
The Daimyō runs off searching for him singing sadly that he
has been tricked.

BAKUCHI JŪŌ 博奕十王   I
(A Gambler Beats the King of Hell)   和

Shite   GAMBLER

26

Ado   EMMA, THE KING OF HELL
Tachishū   DEMONS

Emma, the King of Hell, brings his Demons out to the Crossing of the Six Roads to catch sinners and throw them into Hell. All the sinners have been going to Heaven recently because of the numerous new religions and Hell is in a rather sad state of affairs.

A Gambler comes along, is caught by the Demons and brought before Emma. The Gambler convinces Emma that gambling is fun and not at all sinful. Emma asks for a demonstration since he has never even seen anyone gamble. Since two are necessary for gambling, Emma agrees to bet. The Gambler throws the dice and Emma loses again and again till he has lost all his tools and clothes. Finally the Gambler forces Emma to show him the way to Heaven in order to get his things back. Emma leads the Gambler to Heaven sad that he has lost another sinner.

BAKURŌ 馬口労
(Bakurō, the Horse Trainer)

I
和

Shite   BAKURŌ
Ado   EMMA, THE KING OF HELL

Emma, the King of Hell, has come upon hard days as a result of all the religions which help sinners get to Heaven. Things have gotten so bad that he himself has finally come out to the Crossing of the Six Roads to catch sinners and chase them to Hell.

Bakurō, a Horse Trainer, appears. Emma catches him and

27

accuses him of all sorts of cruelty to animals. Bakurō's plea that he was not cruel at all, but simply trained horses, does him no good. Emma has him well on the way to Hell when he becomes curious about the equipment Bakurō is carrying. Bakurō tells him that with this thing called a bridle, he can tame any horse. Emma asks Bakurō to teach him about horseback riding because it would be very convenient if he could ride around Hell. It would give him more dignity.

They have no horse, so Bakurō talks Emma into playing the part of the horse, puts the bridle on, and mounts him. The tables are turned, and Bakurō takes advantage of the situation by forcing Emma not only to show him the way to Heaven, but to carry him there on his back.

BIKUSADA 比丘貞   I O
(The Aged Nun and Bikusada)   和 大

Shite	NUN
Ado	PARENT
Koado	SON (BIKUSADA)

A Parent takes his Son, who has just reached the age to be named, to an old Nun and asks her to perform the naming ceremony. She is very flattered and pleased that they should ask her to perform this important ceremony. She uses parts of her name and parts of their family name, gives him the name Antarō Bikusada, and presents him with large gifts of rice and gold. The Parent and Son are very pleased.

They begin drinking together in celebration of the occasion, also enjoying themselves with songs and dances. The Parent and Son finally convince the old Nun to dance for them. All three enjoy the happy occasion thoroughly.

BISHAMON 毘沙門 (*See* Bishamon Renga)

BISHAMON RENGA 毘沙門連歌
(The God Bishamon and the Poem)

一 〇
和 大

(Ōkura title: Bishamon 毘沙門)

Shite BISHAMON
Ado MAN I
Koado MAN II

Two Men go to worship at the shrine on Mt. Kurama.
After worshipping they spend the night at the shrine. Man I
has a dream in which he receives a blessed pear. Man II is
jealous, so he pretends he also had a dream in which he was
told the blessed pear was actually for him. Man I, of course,

objects, but Man II is persistent, so Man I says if Man II composes poems with him on the way home, he will give the pear to him.

Bishamon himself appears during their poem-making, cuts the pear in half, gives them one half each, and rewards them further with pieces of his own costume. He asks them to recite the poem they had been composing once more, then they all go off together singing and dancing happily.

In the Ōkura script, Man II does not say he had a dream, but simply insists on a share of the pear. When Bishamon appears, he narrates his life story after which he gives them gifts and they all go off singing about their gifts and blessings. Bishamon does not split the pear, and they do not sing and dance the poem they composed in the first part of the play.

BŌBŌGASHIRA 茫々頭 (*See* Kiku no Hana)

BONSAN 盆山 (The Dwarf Tree Thief)　　I　O
　　　　　　　　　　　　　　　　　　　　　　和　大

| Shite | THIEF |
| Ado | DWARF TREE OWNER |

A Thief, who is not really a thief at all but just a man who is indignant because his friend, who owns many dwarf trees, won't give him even one, breaks into the Dwarf Tree Owner's house to steal one or two.

The Owner hears noises and comes running. The Thief hides behind one of the dwarf trees. The Owner laughs when he sees this big man (who he immediately recognizes as the friend who is always begging for one of the trees) hiding behind such a little tree, and decides to give him a fright and tease him.

First he says that though he thought it was a man, it seems to be a dog. If it is a dog, it will howl. The Thief howls. The Owner says when he looks closer it isn't a dog, but a monkey. If it is a monkey, it will scratch itself and chatter. The Thief scratches himself and chatters. The Owner looks again and says it isn't a monkey at all, but a sea-bream (*tai*). If it's a sea-bream, it will put up its fin. The Thief uses his fan to look like a fin. The Owner says after it puts up its fin, a sea-bream (*tai*) always crys. The Thief doesn't know what to do this time because he has never heard a fish cry, so he goes skipping off shouting, "Tai, tai, tai, tai!" The Owner chases off after him.

In the Ōkura script, the Owner says it is a monkey, then a dog. Only the order is different.

BŌ SHIBARI 棒縛 (Tied to a Stick) I O
和 大

Shite	TARŌ KAJA
Ado	MASTER
Koado	JIRŌ KAJA

Tarō Kaja and Jirō Kaja are great *saké* lovers and their Master has heard that they always steal his *saké* and get drunk when he is away from the house. He has hit upon a plan to prevent their getting to the *saké* this time. He calls Jirō Kaja and asks for his cooperation in tricking Tarō Kaja and tying him to a pole. Jirō Kaja reluctantly agrees and they call Tarō

Kaja and ask him to demonstrate the use of the pole in self-defense. He is very proud of his ability in this art and while he is completely absorbed in his demonstration, they catch his hands and tie them to the pole across the back of his neck. Jirō Kaja is enjoying Tarō Kaja's plight when the Master sneaks up behind him and ties his hands behind his back. He explains the reason for what he has done and goes out on some business or other.

Tied up in this manner, they find they are even thirstier than usual, and decide to go to the *saké* cellar and at least smell the *saké*. This makes them still thirstier. Tarō Kaja hits upon an idea, gets a huge *saké* cup and ladles some *saké* out, tries to drink it, but since he can't get it to his mouth, holds it for Jirō Kaja to drink. When it comes Tarō Kaja's turn to drink, he ladles the *saké*, then puts the full cup in Jirō Kaja's hands (which are tied behind his back), gets down on his knees and drinks.

They get very drunk and are singing and dancing when the Master comes home. He comes up behind them and they see his reflection in the *saké* cup on the floor between them. Thinking it is a hallucination, they make up an insulting song about the Master.

The Master chases them out of the *saké* cellar in a rage.

In the Ōkura script, the Master calls Tarō Kaja and asks him to cooperate in tying Jirō Kaja up. It is Tarō Kaja's idea to have Jirō Kaja perform with the stick and to tie him to it. The Master does not explain why he has tied them up, but they immediately guess the reason after he leaves. In the end the Master chases Tarō Kaja off, then threatens to beat Jirō Kaja, but Jirō Kaja gets loose and chases the Master off with his stick. The rest is the same as the Izumi script.

32

BUAKU 武悪 (Buaku, the Living Ghost)

Shite	BUAKU
Ado	MASTER
Koado	TARŌ KAJA

The Master comes on in a rage calling for Tarō Kaja. He orders Tarō Kaja to go kill his servant Buaku, because he is lazy and impudent, and hasn't been to work for some time. Tarō Kaja pleads for Buaku's life because they were raised together and are good friends. The Master threatens to kill Tarō Kaja if he doesn't carry out this order immediately, so Tarō Kaja accepts the sword and starts out for Buaku's house.

Tarō Kaja has warned Buaku about his behavior many times, but to no avail. If he tells Buaku the truth, he is sure Buaku will stall and make excuses, so he hides the sword and invites Buaku to go fishing with him. He says he will offer the fish to their Master and say they are a gift from Buaku.

33

Since Buaku is especially fond of fishing, he readily agrees.

Tarō Kaja tries to kill Buaku while they are fishing, but Buaku stops him and asks the reason. Tarō Kaja explains that he has made excuses for Buaku time and again, but this time the Master was so angry that he threatened Tarō Kaja with his life if he didn't go to kill Buaku. Even so Buaku accuses him of betrayal, and says that he doesn't blame their Master but Tarō Kaja. He sits down and offers himself to be killed, weeping all the while.

Tarō Kaja, won over by the tears of his old friend, puts away his sword and lets Buaku go, making him promise to leave the country immediately and forever. Buaku asks Tarō Kaja to take care of his wife and children, thanks him profusely for saving his life, and goes happily on his way.

Tarō Kaja reports to his Master that the deed is done. The Master is very happy and asks how Buaku died. Tarō Kaja says that Buaku was expecting it and immediately said his prayers and offered his neck to the sword. Since Buaku died so bravely, the Master is a little sad he acted so hastily, so he decides to go pray for Buaku's soul.

The Master and Tarō Kaja set out for Higashiyama and on the way, as they are crossing Toribeno, they run into Buaku who is on his way to Kiyomizu Temple to pay his respects and express his gratitude before leaving town. He hides as soon as he sees the Master, but it is too late. The Master is sure he saw Buaku, but Tarō Kaja assures him that that is impossible because Buaku is dead, and offers to go see who or what it was.

He finds Buaku scared out of his wits and instructs him to fix himself up like a ghost and appear again.

Tarō Kaja comes back and reports that there is no one in sight, and says that he thinks it must have been Buaku's ghost.

The Master is frightened and wants to start back home, but before they have taken a step, Buaku appears again, this time as a ghost.

The Master orders Tarō Kaja to ask him who he is and what he is doing here to which he answers that he is Buaku's ghost. The Master says he wants to ask him a few questions and orders him to come nearer but not too near. He asks if there is a heaven and a hell to which Buaku answers in the affirmative. He asks if Buaku has met anyone he knows in the other world. Buaku answers that he has met many people he knows including the Master's dead father, and that the father is in purgatory because he was neither bad nor good on earth. He adds that he has a message from the Master's father.

The Master is eager to hear from his father, so Buaku says that the father needs a sword because there are thieves in the other world too, a dagger because he has to attend ceremonies at the court of Emma, the King of Hell, and a fan because he is still practicing singing (in the Ōkura script the father wants the fan because it is very hot even in purgatory). The Master gladly gives Buaku all these things to take to his father. Buaku says the father also instructed him to bring the Master to see him, to which the Master answers that he must stay on earth to pray for the soul of his father and Buaku. At this the Master runs off with Buaku close at his heels exclaiming, "But your father ordered me to take you to see him!"

BUNZŌ 文蔵 I O
(The Tricky Memory Trick) 和 大

Shite	MASTER
Ado	TARŌ KAJA

35

Tarō Kaja took off work for a few days without his Master's permission and went to the capital. His Master heard that he had come back the previous night and goes to his house in a rage. When the Master hears where Tarō Kaja has been and that while there he visited the Master's uncle, he says he will forgive Tarō Kaja if he tells him about the trip and especially about what the uncle gave him to eat, since the uncle is famous for serving very delicious and unusual foods.

Tarō Kaja says he did indeed eat something that was very unusual and very delicious, but he can't recall what it was called. He can only remember that he ate it in the morning. The Master names all the foods he can think of that might be served in the morning, but nothing rings any bells with Tarō Kaja.

Tarō Kaja always has a hard time remembering things, so the Master had instructed him to use the memory trick of relating things. Tarō Kaja says that he remembers that the name of the food is in the chanted narrative (*katari*) the Master likes to recite about the battle at Ishibashi Mountain.

The Master agrees to recite it, but says for Tarō Kaja to stop him when he hears the key word. Tarō Kaja finally stops him on the very last line when he hears the word Bunzō, the name of a warrior. The Master objects that he couldn't have eaten a man, and suddenly realizes that Tarō Kaja has even used a mistaken memory trick. The Master asks him if it was *unzō gayu* (a lukewarm tasteless soup eaten by Zen priests for breakfast) and Tarō Kaja exclaims, "Yes, that's it." The Master scolds him for putting him to so much trouble to recall something so disagreeable.

BUSSHI 仏師 (The Fake Sculptor)　　I O
和 大

| Shite | SCULPTOR OF BUDDHIST IMAGES |
| Ado | COUNTRY MAN |

A Country Man sets out for the capital to buy a Buddhist image for the new shrine he has built, but when he arrives, he remembers that he doesn't know where a Sculptor lives or what one looks like, so he decides to shout as he walks along the streets that he wants to find a sculptor and buy a statue. A dishonest Sculptor hears the Country Man and decides to trick him out of his money. He claims that he is the only true Sculptor of a long line of famous sculptors.

The Country Man asks to see a sample. The Sculptor replys that he has no samples, but does his work according to the specifications and desires of the customer. They discuss the different possibilities and finally decide on a style. As for size they decide on one the size of the Sculptor. When asked

when it will be finished, the Sculptor says it will take three years three months and ninety days. The Country Man asks if it can be done a little sooner and the Sculptor answers that if he is in a hurry, it can be done the next day. If he makes it himself, it will take three years, but if he has his students do it, it can be done by the next day at the same time. They discuss the price and place for the statue to be received and part till the next day.

The Sculptor has never carved so much as a tooth-pick, so he decides to put on a mask, pose as the statue himself, then run away as soon as he has the money in his pocket.

The statue is in an alcove when the Country Man comes. He looks at it, admires its life-like features, but isn't quite satisfied. He asks for it to be changed time and again till finally the Sculptor gets confused, leaves the mask on the side of his head, and is discovered by the Country Man. The Country Man realizes he has been tricked, gets angry, and chases the Sculptor off.

BUSU 附子 (The Delicious Fatal Poison)　　I　O
　　　　　　　　　　　　　　　　　　　　　　　　和　大

Shite	TARŌ KAJA
Ado	MASTER
Koado	JIRŌ KAJA

The Master leaves Tarō Kaja and Jirō Kaja in the house and goes out on some business or other telling them that there is a fatal poison called Busu in a certain container, and that if they so much as get in the breeze that blows across it, they will die immediately.

After the Master leaves, Tarō Kaja gets very curious about what the Busu looks like and talks the very reluctant Jirō Kaja into fanning the breeze in the opposite direction while he takes a look at this fatal poison. When he gets the lid off and sees it, he notices that it looks and smells as though it would be good to eat, so he decides to taste it. Ever cautious Jirō Kaja tries to stop him, but he persists and finds that it is only dark sugar (sugar was extremely scarce in the Muromachi Period, thus it was considered quite a treasure). Jirō Kaja joins him and before they know it, they have eaten it all up.

They wonder what they should do because the Master will surely punish them severely when he finds his precious sugar all gone. Tarō Kaja hits upon an idea, has Jirō Kaja tear the hanging scroll, then helps him break a valuable tea cup.

When the Master returns, they are both weeping inconsolably. He asks them what is wrong and they tell him that they decided to wrestle to kill time. During the match one of them happened to grab the hanging scroll and tore it, then the other fell right on top of the tea cup and smashed it to bits. Since both were the Master's prized possessions, they were sure he would kill them both for destroying them, so they decided to die by eating the poison. They sing a song about how they ate and ate till it was all gone, but it didn't take effect, so here they are.

The Master chases them off in a rage.

CHASANBAI 茶子味梅　　　　　　　Ⅰ
(An International Marriage Problem)　　和

Shite	CHINESE HUSBAND
Ado	JAPANESE WIFE

Koado FRIEND OF WIFE

A Japanese Wife is having trouble with her Chinese Husband, so she goes to ask a Friend for advice. She explains that they have been married for ten years and that her Husband understands Japanese and she understands Chinese quite well, but recently he has been saying some things she doesn't understand, then he begins to cry. The Friend interprets the words for her. The first is a poem expressing his longing for his former Chinese wife and the other is that he wants to drink *saké*.

The Wife is angry at his desire for another woman, but the Friend quiets her down and assures her that if she gives her Husband plenty of *saké*, she will regain his favor.

She returns home and gives her Husband *saké*. This makes him somewhat happier, but he still pines for his former wife. She scolds at him about this, he gets angry and picks up a stick to beat her, she grabs the stick from him and chases him off with it.

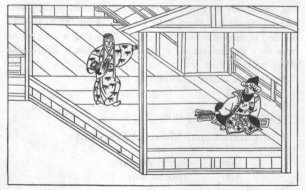

CHA TSUBO 茶壺 (The Tea Box)

Shite	SHYSTER
Ado	COUNTRY MAN
Koado	ARBITER

A Country Man is staggering drunkenly along with a box of tea on his back. He has just purchased his master's supply of tea for the year and got drunk in celebration of the deal on the tea dealer's *saké*. He decides to lie down by the road to sleep for a while, and loosens one of the shoulder straps on the tea box to be more comfortable.

A Shyster happens along the same road and decides to cheat the Country Man out of his tea. He lies down and puts his own arm through the loose strap. He pretends to wake up at the same time as the Country Man and they quarrel over the ownership of the tea box.

An Arbiter comes out to settle the dispute. The Shyster manipulates the questioning so that the Country Man always has to speak first. He eavesdrops and imitates every word and action of the Country Man when it comes his turn to be questioned.

Finally the Arbiter orders them to recite their answers in a song and dance which they must both do simultaneously. The Shyster, still imitating, is about three quarters of a beat behind through the whole recitation.

The Arbiter still cannot make up his mind, and says that when no decision can be made, the goods go to the arbiter. He picks up the tea box and makes a run for it. The Shyster and the Country Man chase after him shouting that they have been cheated.

41

CHIDORI 千鳥 (Catching Plovers)

Shite	TARŌ KAJA
Ado	MASTER
Koado	SAKÉ SHOP OWNER

The Master orders Tarō Kaja to go get a barrel of *saké* for the festival which is the next day. Tarō Kaja reminds him that he already has a big *saké* bill, but the Master insists that he get it somehow or other.

The Saké Shop Owner is determined not to be tricked this time. Tarō Kaja, first of all, talks him into filling the barrel by telling him that several loads of rice are on their way from his Master to pay the bill. The Owner insists that Tarō Kaja wait to leave until the rice arrives.

The Owner always enjoys hearing about Tarō Kaja's trips and adventures, so Tarō Kaja tells him about some children he saw recently catching plovers on a beach. He gets the

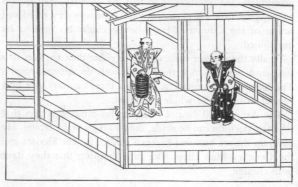

owner to participate in the story in the form of a song and dance game. He tries to get away with the *saké* barrel by using it as a net, then as a plover. The Owner tires of this game soon, so Tarō Kaja begins to demonstrate horseback archery using the barrel as a target. He finally grabs the barrel and runs off. The Owner curses his luck at being tricked once more and chases out after Tarō Kaja.

In the Ōkura script, the Master is going to have a party the same day for which he needs the *saké*. Tarō Kaja pretends he had the price of one barrel of *saké* which he planned to bring to the Sake Shop Owner, but since he can't find it, he decides he must have left it on a shelf at home. Tarō Kaja tells a story about hoeing in the mountains after the one about plovers, so there are three stories and games. The rest is the same as the Izumi script.

CHIGIRIGI 千切木 (Cautious Bravery)　　I　O
和 大

Shite	MAN (TARŌ)
Ado	HOST
Koado	TARŌ KAJA
Tachishū	SEVERAL POETS (GUESTS OF ADO)
Koado	WOMAN (WIFE OF TARŌ)

Several friends gather at the Host's house to have a *renga* (a kind of connected poem) making meeting. One named Tarō usually attends the meetings, but he is not only poor at composing, but is also so noisy that he disturbs the whole gathering making it impossible for the others to enjoy themselves, so they have made it a point to avoid letting him know about the meeting.

Tarō has somehow heard about their meeting in spite of their attempts to keep it from him, and barges in just when they have begun to enjoy themselves. He begins by noisily criticizing everything he sees. The Host has Tarō Kaja ask Tarō to leave, but he insists on staying and continues his noisy criticism. The Host calls Tarō aside and explains clearly that if he is there no one can compose poems properly, so if Tarō will go home quietly, they will call him when the meal is served. He still objects, so the Host throws him out bodily. Still he comes right back in as noisy as ever. They all get up together, take him out to the street, throw him down, kick and beat him.

He lies there crying for help. His Wife has heard about his treatment and comes running. He lies there on the ground crying, "Don't kick me again! I promise not to come anymore!" His Wife shouts, "It's me, you fool! Pull yourself together and get up!"

Tarō gets up quickly, and asks his Wife what she is doing here. She says she heard he was being kicked and beaten. He says no man worth his salt would allow himself to be kicked. She retorts, "Then what are those sandal prints all over your clothes?" He says that since he doesn't have a family seal, all his friends decided on the mark of the sandal sole for him. This makes his Wife even angrier. She insists that he take revenge by killing all those who kicked him. He says, "You mean I should kill everyone who kicks me?" She says, "Of course, if you're a man!" He says, "But it's not the first time!" She says that this is the time to put a stop to people kicking him, hands him a stick and orders him to go take revenge. He says that he might be killed. She says it's better for a man to be killed than to lose his honor. He says, "You go then. I don't care how much I'm kicked, I don't want to die!" She says that if he doesn't take proper revenge, she won't let him in the house. He finally agrees to go, but insists she go along.

They start on their mission. He tells her to get out of the way when they reach the house of the Host and calls politely at the door. She says, "This is no time to be polite! Stomp right in!" He says she is a woman and doesn't know about these things. He calls again and the Host answers, "No one home!" Tarō says, "If there's no one home, then come out and fight like a man!" They go to each house and the same thing happens each time. Tarō is very frightened, each time till the man in the house says, "No one home." But then he becomes very brave and his threats get bigger each time. His Wife, even though she has had to push him along each step of the way, is very impressed with his bravery and in the end coyly invites him to come home with her. They go off happily singing together about the cowardice of the other men and Tarō's bravery.

CHIGO YABUSAME 児流鏑馬 (The Horseback Archery Ceremony Defiled)

Shite	MASTER OF CEREMONIES FOR THE FESTIVAL
Ado	WIFE (OF SHITE)
Koado	TWO HORSEMEN
Koado	HORSE
Tachishū	HEAD AND MANY OTHER WORSHIPPERS

The Master of Ceremonies is in a fix because he has no young boy to play the main part of the Child (Chigo) in the horseback archery exhibition in the festival. He finally talks his Wife into playing the part. The only problem is that she has a tiny baby and there is no one to take care of it during the ceremony, so she decides to wrap it up and hide it in the breast of her costume.

The Head Worshipper on his way to the ceremony explains that when the Child hits the mark with his arrow, it is a sign there will be a good harvest, and if he misses, it is always a bad year. He gathers his fellow Worshippers and they start out for the festival. On their way, they stop by the market in the forest where they admire the various wares and buy what they like. Then they proceed to the ceremonial grounds of the festival.

They all watch the ceremony with great interest and much comment. Everything goes well, the mark is hit and all are happy. After the ceremony, it is customary to take the Child to the temple, have him drink the sacred *saké* and each person in the village thanks him.

The Master of Ceremonies says that the Child cannot drink. The Head Worshipper says he must because it is the custom. The Master of Ceremonies says all right but he must be allowed to keep his hat on. The Head says this is impossible because he must enter the temple where no hats are allowed.

The Worshippers all arm themselves and fight with the Master of Ceremonies. He is winning, but the Head of the Worshippers finally slips around him, takes the hat off the Child, and finds it is the Master of Ceremonies' Wife. All chase the Master of Ceremonies and his Wife off cursing them for defiling the festival.

CHIKUBUSHIMA MAIRI 竹生島詣
(The Pilgrimage to Chikubu Island)

Shite	TARŌ KAJA
Ado	MASTER

Tarō Kaja took a few days off work without his Master's permission. His Master heard that he had returned the previous night and goes to his house in a rage. When asked where he has been, he says he went on a pilgrimage to the shrine on Chikubu Island. His Master promises to forgive him if he will tell about his trip.

Tarō Kaja says that when he got there, several animals were enjoying themselves on the grass making *shūku* (a kind of double entendre riddle) using their own names. There was a dragon, a dog, a monkey, and a serpent. The dragon said, "I have some business to take care of, so I must leave this place" ("dragon" and "leave" are both pronounced *tatsu*). The dog said, "I promised to spend the evening with a friend, so I must leave this place" ("dog" and "to leave" are pronounced *inu* and *inuru*). The monkey said, "I have a guest coming to visit me, so I must leave this place" ("monkey" and "to leave" are both pronounced *saru*). The Master enjoys this story very much, but reminds Tarō Kaja that the serpent is still there. Tarō Kaja can't think of a good way to end the story, so he just says that the serpent slithered into a hole.

The Master scolds him for ruining the story.

DAIHANNYA 大般若
(The Buddhist Sutra and the Shintō Dance)

Shite	PRIEST
Ado	SHRINE MAIDEN
Koado	MAN

A Shrine Maiden of the Shintō religion appears at the Man's house to perform her monthly *kagura* (a Shintō dance of blessing). Before long a Buddhist Priest appears at the same Man's house to read his monthly sutras. The Man places them in separate rooms to perform their services, but before long the Priest begins to complain of the noise of the *kagura* bells and tells the Man to have the Shrine Maiden stop her *kagura* till he is finished with his sutra reading.

The Shrine Maiden objects saying that the *kagura* is more important than the sutras. They argue back and forth for a time, and finally the Priest agrees to try not to pay attention to the noise.

The Priest puts his hands over his ears to keep out the noise. The Shrine Maiden comes and teases him by ringing her bells near his ears. The Priest begins to enjoy the dance and even joins in, forgetting his sutra reading even to the point of using his sutra scroll as bells in mimicking the Shrine Maiden's dance.

DAIKOKU RENGA 大黒連歌
(Daikoku and the Poets)

Shite	DAIKOKU

Ado   WEALTHY MAN
Koado   TARŌ KAJA
Tachishū SEVERAL VILLAGERS

Every year at the time of the Mouse (*ne*) Festival, a group of Villagers gathers at a Wealthy Man's house to celebrate and pray for good fortune for the coming year by composing *renga* (a kind of linked poem). They are gathered together and are in the process of poem making when a stranger appears. When asked to identify himself, he explains that he is Daikoku, the god of the festival. He praises them for their faithful service to him and promises them all prosperity. Then he dances and sings the poem they have composed and gives them gifts.

In the Ōkura script, two Worshippers go to the Daikoku Shrine on Mt. Hiei. They pray, then compose a *renga*. Daikoku appears to them, identifies himself, and tells them his life story in chanted narrative form (*katari*). He asks them to recite the *renga* they had composed once more. They sing the *renga* and dance together. Daikoku rewards the Worshippers with gifts and blessings.

DOBU KACHIRI 井礑 (Plunk! Click!) I O
和大

Shite   BLIND MAN
Ado   KIKUICHI (SHITE'S SERVANT, ALSO BLIND)
Koado   PASSER-BY

A Blind Man calls his servant Kikuichi, who is also blind, to get ready to accompany him on a trip to the capital and

especially to remember to bring along plenty of *saké*.

They have gone some distance when they reach a river. Since there is no bridge, they must wade across. They test the depth of the water by throwing pebbles. When it makes a plunking sound (*dobu*) it is too deep, but they finally find a place where it makes a clicking sound (*kachiri*) which means it has hit the rocks on the bottom immediately, thus the river is shallow at this point.

The Blind Master insists that Kikuichi carry him across on his back, so Kikuichi gets ready. A Passer-by comes along just at this time and decides to take advantage of the situation. The Passer-by jumps on Kikuichi's back, and Kikuichi, unaware of what has happened, carries him across the river. The Blind Master has by this time gotten impatient and begins to shout at Kikuichi not to be so lazy. Kikuichi responds that he has just carried the Master across and asks why he has gone back across. The Master explains that he has been standing in the same spot the whole time. Kikuichi, bewildered but

50

obedient, goes back and on the way back across, this time with his Blind Master on his back, he slips and falls and they both get drenched.

They struggle on across together, and when they reach the other side drenched and chilled through, they decide to have a few drinks to warm themselves up a bit. The Passer-by again takes advantage of them. Every time Kikuichi pours sake for his Master, the Passer-by sticks his own cup under the mouth of the *saké* jug, thus the Master gets none. The Master scolds Kikuichi for spilling all the *saké* on the ground. Kikuichi pours again, this time using up all the *saké*, which the Passer-by receives and drinks again.

The Blind Master and Kikuichi begin accusing each other of drinking all the *saké* and get into a violent quarrel. The Passer-by begins pulling their ears and pinching their noses which causes them to go at each other in earnest. The Passer-by steps to one side and enjoys their fight so much that he finally laughs out loud. They realize what has happened and join forces to catch him. Even so they keep catching and beating each other instead of the culprit as they chase off after him.

In the Ōkura script, Kikuichi convinces his Master to recite a chanted narrative (*katari*) before they reach the river. After the Passer-by has enjoyed himself, he leaves quietly. The Master and Kikuichi continue fighting. Kikuichi finally throws his Master down and runs off saying, "I've won! I've won! I've won!" The Master picks himself up and shouts after him, "Treat your Master like this and you will have a black future!" The rest is the same as the Izumi script. The Ōkura title is pronounced Dobu Katchiri.

51

DOCHI HAGURE どちはぐれ
(A Day Wasted for Want of a Decision)

I
和

Shite	PRIEST
Ado	MAN I
Koado	MAN II

A Priest is invited to preach one place where he will receive a large sum of money and there is another place he goes every month on this day where he is royally fed. He argues with himself about which place to go so long that it is finally to late to go either place. He goes off philosophizing about greed, lack of decision, etc.

DOMORI 吃り (The Stutter)

I O
和 大

Shite	MAN (TARŌ)
Ado	WOMAN
Koado	ARBITER

Tarō and his Wife are in the middle of a fight. She is beating him unmercifully with a stick and shouting accusations at the top of her lungs. The Arbiter trys to stop the fight. Tarō tells the Arbiter he can't take it any longer and he wants a divorce. The Wife says, "All right, but give me back my dowry clothes, bedding, and furniture." Tarō stutters so badly that he can't defend himself properly, but says that if he sings, he doesn't stutter. The Arbiter has him put his complaints and explanations into a song. In the song he explains what a terrible Wife she is and how meager her dowry was. The Wife begins shouting again and chases him off.

52

DONDARŌ 鈍太郎 (*See* Dontarō)

DONGONGUSA 鈍根草
(The Foolroot Weed)

I
和

Shite	TARŌ KAJA
Ado	MASTER

It is September, and time for the Master to make his annual pilgrimage to the Kurama Shrine. He calls Tarō Kaja to go with him. They pray, then proceed to the priest's house they always visit. The priest is busy and can't see them, but sends some Foolroot Weed for them to eat. The Master refuses to eat it saying he doesn't want to become foolish, so Tarō Kaja is happy to eat it all. The Master sees some Smart Weed in the garden, has Tarō Kaja pick some for him and eats it.

They start on their way home. The Master forgets his sword in the room, and Tarō Kaja picks it up and hides it behind his back. Before they have gone far, the Master notices that his sword is missing and tries to send Tarō Kaja back for it. Instead of going to get the sword, Tarō Kaja tells a long story about the origin of Foolroot Weed and Smart Weed and ends by saying that neither has any effect. In proof of this, he says the Master ate Smart Weed and forgot his sword, but Tarō Kaja ate Foolroot Weed and not only didn't forget anything but picked up something. When asked what he picked up, he produces the sword.

The Master scolds Tarō Kaja for making fun of him.

DONTARŌ 鈍太郎

(Dontarō's Method for Handling Women)

(Ōkura title: Dontarō)

Shite	DONTARŌ
Ado	WIFE
Koado	MISTRESS

Dontarō has been away from the capital for three years and during this time has made a fortune, but has not corresponded with his family at all. He is now on his way home and worried about the reaction of his family, but confident they will be happy when they see the fortune he has brought with him.

He reaches his Wife's house, but when he asks to be allowed to enter, his Wife doesn't believe it is really him, and says she has taken a man who fights with a stick as her husband, and if Dontarō tries to get in, he will be beaten by her new husband.

At this Dontarō is unhappy on the one hand because he was anxious to see his son, but happy on the other hand, because now he is free of his ugly Wife and can go to live with his beautiful Mistress. He goes to his Mistress's house and gets the same treatment. His Mistress says she has taken a halberd expert as her new husband.

Dontarō decides it is useless to fight or beg any longer, so he decides to give up his secular life and become a monk. He makes this decision and goes off to put it into effect.

The next morning the Wife and the Mistress both discover their mistake. They both actually did not believe it was Dontarō because the children in their respective neighborhoods had often played tricks on them saying Dontarō had

54

come home. Both assume he is now at the other house, so they both leave their own homes at the same time to go apologize and make their peace with Dontarō. They run into each other on the way, explain to each other what they have done, and decide that the rumor, which they have both heard, that Dontarō is going to become a monk, must be true. They are sure he will pass this particular spot, so they decide to wait together and try to persuade him to forgive them and change his mind.

Dontarō appears, lamenting his fate and reciting sutras through his tears. He pretends not to recognize the Wife and Mistress when they try to stop him, saying that his Wife and Mistress have both taken other men while he was gone, so they must be someone else's wife and mistress.

The Wife pleads with him explaining that the two have united their efforts to get him back. Dontarō answers that if this uniting of efforts means they will accept each other and not give him any more trouble, he will come back. They readily agree.

Dontarō says, "All right, I will stay with my Mistress twenty-five days of the month and with my Wife five days of the month (Ōkura script twenty and ten days). His Wife immediately objects angrily. He begins reciting sutras again. The Mistress then pleads with him saying, "Yes, that is quite unfair. Please come back and stay half the month in each place." The Wife agrees, but insists that the first half of the month must be at her place. Dontarō says that he is the one to decide which half where, and if his decision is not satisfactory he won't return. He begins reciting sutras again.

They both plead again saying they will agree to anything he says. He says if that is the case he will spend the first fifteen days of the month with his Mistress and the last fifteen days of the month with his Wife. He commands them to make a chair with their hands and carry him home on it. Then he makes up a song stating that this is the Hand Chair of Sir Dontarō and orders them to sing it loudly as they go along. They carry him off in a state of agreement and family bliss.

EBISU BISHAMON 夷毘沙門 I O
(Ebisu and Bishamon) 和 大

Shite	EBISU
Ado	WEALTHY MAN
Koado	BISHAMON

A wealthy man has a beautiful daughter for whom he wants to find a suitable husband. He puts up a notice advertising this fact and both Ebisu and Bishamon come in response. They each tell of their own qualifications and the bad points of the

other in a chanted narrative (*katari*). They make gifts of the things they have and are wearing to the Wealthy Man while singing and dancing. All ends on a felicitous note with no decision as to which will be the new husband.

EBISU DAIKOKU 夷大黒　　　　Ｉ　Ｏ
(Ebisu and Daikoku) 　　　　　　　和　大

Shite	DAIKOKU
Ado	VILLAGER
Koado	EBISU

A Villager from Katano village in Kōchi, on his way home after a pilgrimage to the Shrines of Daikoku on Mount Hiei and Ebisu in Nishinomiya, is stopped in front of his own home by two strangers who identify themselves as Ebisu and Daikoku, the gods. He invites them in. They praise him for his faithful service and each tells about himself in a chanted narrative (*katari*). They they bless him with gifts, song and dance.

In the Ōkura script, the Villager is from Tsu.

ECHIGO MUKO 越後聟　　　　　Ｉ
(The Groom from Echigo) 　　　　和

Shite	GROOM FROM ECHIGO
Ado	FATHER-IN-LAW
Koado	TARŌ KAJA
Third Ado	BLIND GROOM

A Father-in-law, who has many daughters, is preparing for the ceremonial first visit of the Groom of one of his daughters who is from Echigo. The Blind Groom of one of the older daughters arrives to participate in the ceremony.

The Groom from Echigo arrives. After the ceremonial greetings, *saké* is served. As usual, singing and dancing follows with the Father-in law dancing first. Next they convince the Blind Groom to dance. Then the Groom from Echigo agrees to perform the famous Echigo Lion Dance. While he is putting on the costume for this dance, the Father-in-law convinces the Blind Groom to recite part of the Heike Story (a chanted narrative, recited to the accompaniment of the Biwa, known by all blind men of the *kōtō* class). The Echigo Groom then dances the Lion Dance for which his country is famous. With this the ceremony and celebration are successfully completed.

FUJI MATSU 富士松 (The Fuji Pine)　　I　O
和　大

Shite　　　TARŌ KAJA
Ado　　　　MASTER

Tarō Kaja took a few days off work without his Master's permission and made a trip to Mount Fuji. His Master heard that he had come back the previous night and brought a fine Fuji pine tree with him. He goes to Tarō Kaja's house determined to get the tree from him. Tarō Kaja pretends that the tree belongs to someone else. The Master offers to trade his hawk or his horse, but Tarō Kaja says that the owner of the tree has no use for such things.

The Master orders Tarō Kaja to accompany him to the shrine. On the way the Master orders Tarō Kaja to compose poems with him and if he fails, he must give the Master the pine tree. Tarō Kaja is so good at these poems (*renga*) that the Master tires of them by the time they reach the shrine and reluctantly allows Tarō Kaja to keep his pine tree.

FUKITORI 吹取 (To Flute for a Wife)　　I O
　　　　　　　　　　　　　　　　　　　　　　　　　和 大

Shite	MAN
Ado	FRIEND
Koado	WOMAN

A Man has been to the Kiyomizu Temple to pray for a wife and was told in a dream to go to the Gojō Bridge at midnight on the night of the full moon and play a flute and his new wife would appear. He has never played a flute in his life, so he asks a Friend who is a very good flute player to go with him and play the flute in his place.

The Friend has planned to go moon viewing, so he refuses. The Man pleads with the Friend and he finally consents, but when they get to the bridge, the Friend is so interested in looking at the moon, its reflection in the water, etc., that the Man begins to worry that the night will be gone before the Friend plays for him. The Friend finally plays and the Woman appears.

The Woman seems to prefer the Friend. The Man tries to convince her that she belongs to him until he gets her veil off and finds how ugly she is. The Man says since she likes his Friend so much, the Friend should take her. The Friend claims he already has a wife and runs off. The Man tells the Woman that the one who played the flute is her "intended husband." She says, "No! It's you!" He tries to run away and she chases off after him.

In the Ōkura script the Shite is a Flute Player and the Ado is a Woman, only two characters. The Flute Player comes to the bridge every night where he plays his flute till dawn. The last few nights a strange Woman has been appearing and requesting various songs which he has played for her. He has decided to find out who she is tonight. When she appears, he asks her to take off her veil, and she refuses. He pulls it off her, discovers she is actually a fox in disguise, and chases her off.

FUKUBE NO SHIN　福部の神
(The Gourd God and Tarō)

I
和

Shite	TARŌ
Ado	GOURD BEATER PRIEST
Tachishū	GOURD BEATERS
Koado	GOURD GOD

Tarō is a kind of priest known as a gourd beater because their prayers and incantations are performed to the accompaniment of a gourd which they tap with a stick. Tarō has come on hard times and decides to give up gourd beating and try his luck at some other trade. He goes to the temple to inform the god of his intentions and pay his respects. He spends the night at the temple, and while he is sleeping, the Gourd God appears to him and promises that if he continues his present trade, he will become successful, but if he takes up some other trade, he will surely fail. The God leaves him a fine priest's robe and a new gourd.

When Tarō wakes up, he is very happy and puts on the robe. In the meantime, Tarō's fellow Gourd Beaters have heard what he has done and come to search for him to talk him out of his plan. They find him dressed in the new robe. He tells them what has happened and asks them to join him in a thankful dance to celebrate his good fortune. They all beat their gourds, dance and sing for joy.

FUKUBE NO SHIN 福部の神
(The Gourd Beaters) (*See* Hachi Tataki)

FUKUBE NO SHIN TSUTOME IRI
福部の神勤入 (*See* Hachi Tataki)

FUKU NO KAMI 福の神 I O
(The God of Happiness) 和 大

Shite	GOD OF HAPPINESS
Ado	WORSHIPPER I
Koado	WORSHIPPER II

At the end of every year, two Worshippers go the the Grand Shrine at Izumo to pay their respects to the God of Happiness. They are throwing beans while chanting "in with happiness" and "out with devils," when the God of Happiness appears and identifies himself. He asks them if they know how to find happiness and they answer, "With money." He says that it is not money, but the way of life upon which happiness depends. After talking to them, he says he is thirsty and asks for wine which they gladly serve him. He dances and sings a song which tells them that the way to find happiness is to make a happy home with one's wife, get up early, and welcome guests with good wine.

In the Ōkura script, the God of Happiness asks for wine as soon as he appears. The two Worshippers ask him how to find true happiness, and he tells them it is not with money and worldly things, but by having a pure heart. The rest is the same as the Izumi script.

FUKURŌ 梟 (*See* Fukurō Yamabushi)

FUKURŌ YAMABUSHI 梟山伏 I O
(The Hooting Yamabushi)   和 大

Shite	YAMABUSHI (WARRIOR PRIEST)
Ado	OLDER BROTHER
Koado	YOUNGER BROTHER

Older Brother visits a Yamabushi to request incantations for his Younger Brother. Younger Brother has been acting so strange lately that Older Brother fears he has been possessed by something or other.

The Yamabushi agrees to exert all his powers. Soon after the incantations begin, Younger Brother begins hopping around hooting. Older Brother recalls that a few days before, Younger Brother and his friends had gone to the mountains to destroy owl nests. The Yamabushi declares that Younger

Brother is obviously possessed by an owl and doubles his efforts.

During the chanting, hopping, and hooting, Younger Brother accidentally breathes on Older Brother which starts him hopping and hooting too. Finally the Yamabushi succumbs to the spell and they all three go off hopping and hooting merrily.

FUMI NINAI 文荷
(Two to Deliver One Letter)

I O
和 大

Shite	TARŌ KAJA
Ado	MASTER
Koado	JIRŌ KAJA

The Master calls Tarō Kaja and Jirō Kaja and says that he wants a letter delivered to a priest friend of his which says that he will go to visit him that evening. He orders Tarō Kaja to deliver the letter, but he doesn't want to go and suggests that Jirō Kaja be sent. Jirō Kaja doesn't know the way, so the Master orders them both to go.

As they go along the road, they argue about who should carry the letter. They pass it back and forth several times, all the while joking about how their Master seems to have become a religious fanatic, or perhaps it's the priest more than the religion he is interested in, etc. They soon tire of passing it back and forth, so they tie it to a pole and carry it across their shoulders singing as they go along. They become more and more curious about what the letter says. They finally open it, comment on the fact that it is written in the language a man uses when writing to his mistress, and get so excited and are

63

having so much fun reading it that they inadvertently rip it in half. To get rid of the pieces, they begin fanning them while singing a song about a message being delivered on the wings of a breeze.

The Master, worried because they are late, goes out to look for them, and finds them fanning and singing. They try to smooth out the pieces, apologizing profusely, but the Master chases them off in a rage.

In the Ōkura script, the letter is to Sako no Samurō. The discussion about the contents of the letter centers around the idea that the letter uses such words as mountain and ocean. They decide that this is the reason it became so heavy. The rest is the same as the Izumi script.

FUMI YAMADACHI 文山賊   I O
(The Cowardly Bandits)   和 大

(Ōkura title written: 文山立
      Shite   BANDIT I
      Ado   BANDIT II

Two cowardly Bandits quarrel over a misunderstanding in signals. They threaten to kill each other and begin to fight. They stop when they are about to fall into a thorn patch saying that that would hurt too much. They start their fight again and stop when they are about to fall over the edge of a cliff saying that that would break all the bones in a man's body.

Since there are no witnesses, they decide that they will leave a letter to inform the world of their bravery even in death. While writing the letter, they remember their wives, children, and relatives and begin to cry. One suggests they put

off their dying till another day because he is having guests that evening, and the other says that as a matter of fact he has promised to visit a friend the same evening so he too is willing to put it off. Both are relieved because, they admit to each other, neither really wanted to die anyway. They decide to make up, and put off dying indefinitely. They start on their way home hand in hand, singing happily.

FUMIZUMŌ 文相撲   I O 和 大
(Wrestling by the Book)

(Ōkura title pronounced: FUZUMŌ)

    Shite   DAIMYŌ
    Ado   TARŌ KAJA
    Koado SUMŌ WRESTLER

A Daimyō sends his servant Tarō Kaja out to look for a man to hire as a new servant. Tarō Kaja finds a Sumō Wrestler

and brings him home. The Daimyō decides to wrestle with him to test his ability. He uses a throw that the Daimyō doesn't know, so the Daimyō looks it up to find if it is really according to the rules. This happens two or three times till the Wrestler finally gets impatient and throws the Daimyō while he is reading his book of rules. The Daimyō doesn't want to admit defeat, so he throws Tarō Kaja, who has no experience in *sumō*, and goes off declaring, "I've won! I've won!"

In the Ōkura script, the Wrestler wins once, the Daimyō looks up the throw, the Daimyō wins the second time, and when the Wrestler wants one more round the Daimyō tells him he had better write his will. The Wrestler says the Daimyō should write his own. The Wrestler wins the third round and leaves. The rest is the same as the Izumi script.

FUNA WATASHI MUKO　船渡聟
(The Groom in the Boat)

I O
和　大

Shite	GROOM
Ado	BOATMAN FROM YAWASE (FATHER-IN-LAW)
Koado	MOTHER-IN-LAW (BOATMAN'S WIFE)

A newly married Groom goes to make his ceremonial first visit to his Father-in-law's house. On the way he must cross a river, so he calls a boat. The Boatman insists on, and finally threatens the Groom until he agrees to let the Boatman have a drink of the *saké* he is taking as a gift to his Father-in-law. By the time they reach the opposite shore, the Boatman has drunk all the *saké*. The Groom reaches his destination. His Mother-in-law goes to call the Father-in-law who happens to be the Boatman who drank all the *saké*. The Mother-in-law, when she hears this, insists that the Father-in-law shave his beard so the new Groom will not recognize him as the same man (she has, by the way, been trying to talk him into shaving this beard for a long time). The Father-in-law objects, but she finally wins the argument and shaves it for him. But all the fuss has been for nothing, because when the Groom sees the Father-in-law's face, he immediately recognizes him as the Boatman and asks why he has shaved his beard. The Father-in-law apologizes for his misconduct. He is forgiven and they do a song and dance in celebration of the happy occasion.

In the Ōkura script, the Boatman and the Father-in-law are two separate characters and the Mother-in-law does not appear. In her place Tarō Kaja appears. The Groom drinks with the Boatman, and they sing and dance together. When the Groom reaches the Father-in-law's house, he gives the *saké* barrel to Tarō Kaja who discovers it is empty. The Groom is so embarrassed that he runs off. The Father-in-law and Tarō Kaja try to call him back, exclaiming that it doesn't matter that it is empty.

FUNE FUNA 船ふな
(A Pronunciation Problem)

I O
和大

Shite   TARŌ KAJA
Ado   MASTER

The Master calls Tarō Kaja to accompany him on an outing, and they decide to go to Nishinomiya. On the way they come to a river which they must cross by boat. Tarō Kaja calls for a boat using the word *funa* (the word for boat is *fune*, but in compound words such as *funabito*, meaning boatman, the ending *e* changes to *a*). The Master scolds him saying that the proper word is *fune*. Tarō Kaja, whose knowledge of poetry is well known, says that he knows many poems in which the word *funa* is used, but none which use the word *fune*. They compete with poems. The Master uses the same poem at different speeds and with different inflections since he is not well versed in poetry. When Tarō Kaja objects the Master says he knows a song that uses *fune*. He sings his song till he comes to a place where *funa* is also used and says he has forgotten the rest of it. Tarō Kaja finishes it gleefully, and the Master chides him saying, "You could let your Master win an argument once in a while, don't you think?"

FUSE NAI KYŌ 無布施経　　I O
(Sermon Without Donation)　　和　大
(Ōkura title written: 布施無経)

Shite　　HŌKE PRIEST
Ado　　A PARISHIONER

A Priest goes to pay his regular monthly visit to a Parishioner who is in the habit of giving him a regular monthly donation (*fuse*) for his sermons and blessings. The Parishioner for some reason or other forgets to give the Priest his regular donation. The Priest comes back five or six times on the pretense of having forgotten some blessing, some piece of advice, etc. In everything he says he manages to include the word *fuse* meaning "donation" in order to try to jog the Parishioner's memory. In his final attempt, he takes off his *kesa* (a piece of the ceremonial robes), stuffs it into the breast of his kimono and returns, pretending to have dropped it. The Parishioner finally realises the meaning of these repeated visits and brings

out the money. The Priest tries to refuse to accept the money since he has made such a nuisance of himself. He says that he doesn't want it to be thought that the donation was the reason he has come back so many times. The Parishioner forces him to take it by shoving it into the breast of his kimono, thus accidentally pulling out the *kesa* which was so carefully hidden there. The Priest is thus completely found out, apologizes and humbly sets off for home.

FUTARI BAKAMA 二人袴   I O
(Two People in One Hakama)   大 和

    Shite   GROOM
    Ado   FATHER-IN-LAW
    Koado   TARŌ KAJA
    Third Ado   FATHER OF THE GROOM

A Groom prepares to make his ceremonial first visit to his Father-in-law. He is very shy and insists that his Father go with him. His Father goes with him as far as the front gate of the Father-in-law's house and plans to wait there for him. Tarō Kaja sees the Father, informs the Father-in-law, and the Father-in-law asks to see the Father too. They have only brought one *hakama* so the Groom takes it off and the Father puts it on and appears before the Father-in-law. This exchange is performed several times till the Father-in-law finally insists that they appear together. They tear the *hakama* in two and appear with only a half a *hakama* in front of each of them. They perform the ceremony, drink and begin to dance. In the dances, the Father and the Groom never make any turns except when the Father-in-law and Tarō Kaja aren't looking. The

Father-in-law suggests that they all three dance together and while they are dancing, Tarō Kaja discovers that the Father's and the Groom's *hakama* are only half a *hakama* each. They are embarrassed, throw the *hakama* over their faces and run off. The Father-in-law tries to call them back saying that they shouldn't worry about a little thing like that.

FUTARI DAIMYŌ 二人大名 I O
(Two Daimyōs) 和大

Shite	DAIMYŌ I
Ado	DAIMYŌ II
Koado	PASSER-BY

Two Daimyōs go out together, but both of them have no servant to accompany them to carry their swords. On the road they meet a Man of servant class and even though he is in a hurry on important business, they force him into service.

In return the Passer-by threatens them with their own swords, forcing them to hand over not only their daggers, but their clothes as well. They look so comical in their underwear and tall black hats that he next forces them to pretend to be dogs fighting, then roosters fighting, then toys that when pushed over always return to an upright position. While they are rolling around on the ground as toys and singing the song he has taught them, he decides he has had enough fun, so he runs off with their possessions. They chase him off shouting that they have been robbed.

FUZUMŌ 文相撲 (*See* Fumizumō)

GAN DAIMYŌ 雁大名   I
(The Goose Stealing Daimyō)   和

Shite	DAIMYŌ
Ado	TARŌ KAJA
Koado	SHOP OWNER

The Daimyō sends Tarō Kaja to buy some food to entertain guests he has invited that evening. Tarō Kaja goes to the market and finds a goose. The Shop Owner won't allow him to take the goose without paying for it. Tarō Kaja goes back to get money from the Daimyō, but finds there is none to be had. They decide to steal the goose.

The Daimyō goes to the shop and pretends to buy the goose. Tarō Kaja arrives on the scene and complains to the Shop Owner that he has come back with the money and wants his goose. The Shop Owner informs him it is already sold. (The

Daimyō and Tarō Kaja pretend not to know each other.) The Daimyō and Tarō Kaja pretend to fight and the Shop Owner tries to stop then. In the confusion they both grab something and run. Tarō Kaja gets the goose and the Daimyō gets a present for his Wife. They go off chuckling together.

GAN KARIGANE 鴈雁金   I O
(Two Words for Goose)   和 大

Shite	FARMER FROM IZUMI
Ado	FARMER FROM TSU
Ado	TAX COLLECTOR

A Farmer from Izumi and one from Tsu meet on the way to the capital to pay their taxes. The Farmer from Izumi sees that the one from Tsu is taking a goose. This is the same as his own tax, but his is well wrapped so he lies and says he received the package from his lord, and he doesn't know what is in it.

They reach the capital and the Farmer from Izumi goes in to pay his tax first. When he presents the tax, he says he has brought a *gan* (goose). The Farmer from Tsu hears this and is angry that the Farmer from Izumi lied to him before, so when he presents his goose, he says it is a *karigane* (another word for goose).

The Tax Collector calls them in together and asks them why, since they are from neighboring territories, they use different words for goose. They each recite a chanted narrative (*katari*) in which the word they used appears. The Tax Collector praises their cleverness and rewards them with *saké* after which they go off singing and dancing happily together.

GAN TSUBUTE 鴈礫
(A Goose and a Pebble)

Shite   DAIMYŌ
Ado   PASSER-BY
Koado   ARBITER

A Daimyō appears, brags about what a good shot he is with the bow and arrow, and announces he is on his way to a lake to shoot water birds. On the way to the lake, he finds a goose by the road. He shoots at it and misses completely. He decides to hide in the bushes and try another shot. While he is preparing to shoot again, a Man passes by, picks up a pebble, throws it at the goose, and makes a direct hit. He picks up the goose and starts off with it. The Daimyō runs out screaming that it is his goose and the Passer-by has stolen it. The Passer-by refuses to give it up, so the Daimyō threatens to shoot him. The Arbiter appears on the scene, and asks both sides of the

74

story. Seeing that the Daimyō is a very poor shot, he suggests that the goose be put back where it was and the Daimyō be given a chance to shoot at it. If he makes a hit on his first shot, it is his, but if he misses, he loses the goose to the Passer-by. This plan is agreed on. The Daimyō takes a great deal of time in aiming and tries to get close. The Passer-by urges him to hurry. Finally the Daimyō drops his arrow, and the Passer-by grabs the goose and runs off with it. The Daimyō runs off after him shouting, "At least give me a few feathers to make a feather duster!"

GYŪBA 牛馬
(The Race of the Horse and the Cow)

I O
和 大

Shite	SELLER OF COWS
Ado	OFFICIAL IN CHARGE OF THE MARKET
Koado	SELLER OF HORSES

The Official posts a sign saying that the first man to reach the market will be given the best booth and will be named the head of the market. A Horse Seller arrives while it is still dark, makes his claim on the best booth, and decides to sleep till others arrive. A Cow Seller arrives a little later, sees the Horse Seller asleep, and decides to try to trick him out of the position. The Cow Seller pretends to sleep too. They both wake up and begin to argue about who arrived first.

The Official arrives on the scene and puts a stop to the fight. To settle the argument he has them both narrate (*katari*) the virtues of the horse and the cow respectively. Both have such a good story that the Official cannot decide, so he says they must compete for the position. The Horse Seller suggests a race to which the Cow Seller objects, but is finally forced to agree. The Horse Seller jumps on his horse and the Cow Seller on his cow. The horse immediately takes the lead, and the Horse Seller begins to shout that he has won. The Cow Seller, while urging his cow on, shouts, "Don't be so sure, I'll catch up with you by day after tomorrow at this time!"

HACHIKU RENGA　八句連歌
(A Debt Paid with a Poem)

和　大

| Shite | MAN I |
| Ado | MAN II |

Man I is in debt to Man II and is still not able to pay him back, but feels he must at least pay him a visit. When he reaches Man II's house, Man II thinks he has come to borrow more, and claims to be out. As Man I is leaving he sees some beautiful cherry blossoms in the garden and composes the first line of a poem. Man II hears him, and being very fond of composing *renga* (a kind of linked poem), calls him back saying he has just come home, and offers the second line of the poem.

Each line of the poem is, on the surface, about flowers and spring, but has a hidden meaning concerning the debt. In this manner Man I is offering his apology for being late in paying the debt. Man II is so impressed with Man I's ability at poem making that he returns the IOU and says the books are cleared between them. Man I is so happy he can't believe his ears, thanks Man II profusely, and goes off singing happily about his good luck.

In the Ōkura script, Man II goes to Man I's house to dun him for the money he has borrowed. Man I pretends to be out, then leaves by the back gate. Man II guessed that he would try this trick, and catches Man I coming out. Man II forces Man I to come home with him to pay the debt. Man I stalls by admiring various features of Man II's house. Man II finally gives up trying to get money out of Man I, and suggests they compose poems (*renga*). At the end Man I sings happily on his way home as he tears up the IOU. The rest is the same as the Izumi script.

HACHI TATAKI 鉢叩 I O
(The Gourd Beaters) 和 大

(Ōkura titles: Fukube no Shin 福部の神 and Fukube no Shin Tsutome Iri 福部の神勤入

Shite PRIEST I (GOURD BEATER)
Ado PRIEST II (GOURD BEATER)
Tachishū SEVERAL PRIESTS (GOURD BEATERS)
Koado GOURD GOD

A group of Priests of the Gourd God, called Gourd Beaters, go to the temple to pray. Their prayers are accompanied by the beating of gourds and small brass gongs. They make a living by selling tea whisks. Tea whisks have not been selling too well lately, so they are all quite poor. This is the reason for their gathering together to pray.

They pray, chant, beat their gongs and gourds, and perform a ritual dance. The Gourd God appears and blesses them.

In the Ōkura script, the Gourd Beaters are not poor, but simply are making their annual pilgrimage to the Gourd God's temple to thank him for his blessings. Fukube no Shin and Fukube no Shin Tsutome Iri are the same story. The only difference is that the former does not have the ritual dance and song (*tsutome*) of the Gourd Beaters.

HAGI DAIMYŌ 萩大名   I O
(The Daimyō and the Bush Clover   和 大
Blossoms)

Shite	DAIMYŌ
Ado	TARŌ KAJA
Koado	GARDEN OWNER

A country Daimyō has been busy in the capital for several months and decides he needs some recreation. He asks Tarō Kaja for advice on what to do and where to go. Tarō Kaja suggests viewing a garden that he knows of, that has beautiful flowering clover bushes. The price for seeing the garden is the recitation of a poem. The Daimyō is not very well educated and has a very poor memory so Tarō Kaja uses several tricks to help the Daimyō remember the poem he has taught him.

The Daimyō is confident that with the hints Tarō Kaja has arranged, he will be able to recite the poem, but when the time comes, he gets stage fright and forgets everything. He also makes unbelievable mistakes in etiquette. In the middle of the proceedings, Tarō Kaja gets disgusted and goes home. Finally the Garden Owner gets angry and chases the Daimyō out.

HAKUYŌ 伯養
(Hakuyō, the Blind Biwa Borrower)

I O
和 大

Shite	BLIND PRIEST
Ado	HAKUYŌ (BLIND MAN)
Koado	FRIEND (WHO OWNS A BIWA)

On his way to the capital for the yearly gathering of blind men, Hakuyō stops by a Friend's house to borrow his Biwa (an ancient Japanese stringed instrument). Hakuyō cannot play the Biwa, but wants to carry one for the sake of appearance since blind priests carry them.

A Blind Priest whose Biwa is being repaired stops by the same Friend's house on his way to the same gathering to borrow the same Biwa.

The Friend understands the situation, but since he has already promised the Biwa to Hakuyō, he suggests that Hakuyō and the Blind Priest settle the problem between themselves.

The Blind Priest explains his problem to Hakuyō, but Hakuyō refuses to give in. The Friend suggests they compete for the Biwa. They agree and the Blind Priest proposes composing poems. The Blind Priest composes a poem in which he refers to Hakuyō as footwear (*haku* means "to wear on the feet") to which Hakuyō answers angrily with a poem in which

79

he calls the Blind Priest a blind dog. They have both composed equally good poems.

Since the winner can't be decided by the poetry, Hakuyō suggests a *sumō* match. They get ready to wrestle, but can't find each other. The Friend laughs at their plight and offers to bring their hands together so they can get started. Instead of grabbing each other's hands, they each grab one of the Friend's hands, throw him down, and run off, both gleefully claiming they have won the match. The Friend picks himself up and shouts after them that he will lend neither of them his Biwa because of the rough treatment he has suffered.

In the Ōkura script, Hakuyō asks to borrow the Biwa for his teacher because the fourth string of his teacher's Biwa is broken. Hakuyō and the Priest begin to fight before the poem contest is suggested. The order of poems is opposite, Hakuyō first, then the Priest. The rest is the same as the Izumi script.

HANA ARASOI 花争   I O
(The Flower Quarrel)   和 大

Shite	TARŌ KAJA
Ado	MASTER

The Master calls Tarō Kaja and orders him to go along on a flower viewing outing (*hana mi*). Tarō Kaja says that if the Master wants to view a nose (also *hana*), it is not necessary to go out, and offers his own nose to look at. The Master explains that he means flowers (*hana*) not noses (*hana*). Tarō Kaja says that the Master should have said cherry blossom viewing. The Master objects that the proper word is flower viewing (*hana mi*), but Tarō Kaja insists that it is cherry

80

blossom viewing (*sakura mi*) offering to recite an old poem to prove it.

They exchange poems to prove their point until Tarō Kaja slips up by reciting only the first line of a poem in which the word *sakura* is used and the Master adds the second line in which the word *hana mi* appears. Tarō Kaja laughs and says, "Oh, you know that poem too!" The Master scolds him for trying to cheat.

HANAGO 花子 (Visiting Hanago) I O
大
和

Shite	WELL-TO-DO MAN
Ado	WIFE
Koado	TARŌ KAJA

A Well-to-do Man wants very badly to visit his mistress, but can't get out of the house because of his jealous Wife. He

tells her he has been having bad dreams, therefore he must go on a long pilgrimage to pray. She refuses to let him go, but finally gives him permission to sit *zazen* in the chapel for one full night.

He makes her promise not to look in on him, but as a safety measure, he calls Tarō Kaja and forces him to sit *zazen* in his place. The Man then goes happily on his way to his mistress Hanago's house.

The Wife, of course, breaks her promise and looks in on the *zazen* session. (The sitting is done, in this case, with a *kimono* over the head.) She discovers what has happened, and threatening Tarō Kaja with his life if he doesn't cooperate, takes his place to wait for the return of her husband.

The Man returns in a happy drunken daze at dawn, and thinking he is talking to Tarō Kaja asks him to stay covered with the *kimono* while he tells the happenings of the night as he is too shy to talk about it face to face. The Wife listens till she can take no more, and is about to explode when the Man finishes his story and orders Tarō Kaja to take off the *zazen kimono*. The person under the *kimono* refuses, so the Daimyō pulls it off himself and finds the angry face of his Wife. She chases him off in a fit of jealous rage.

HANA NUSUBITO 花盗人 (The Flower Thief)

I O
和 大

    Shite   THIEF
    Ado   GARDEN OWNER

The Garden Owner complains that some of his cherry blossoms were stolen the night before. Since a thief usually returns to the scene of his crime, the Man decides to hide in the garden and ambush the Thief.

Sure enough, the Thief comes back for another branch. The Owner jumps out, catches him, and ties him up. The Thief composes a poem in his sadness. The Garden Owner, also a lover of poems, answers with another poem. They begin enjoying their poetic conversation. The Owner releases the Thief and brings out *saké*. They proceed to get drunk together and become good friends. Finally the Thief gets ready to leave and the Garden Owner presents him with a large branch of cherry blossoms and invites him to come back again soon.

In the Ōkura script, the Garden Owner brings a group of Friends to see his flowers. They discover a branch has been stolen and all wait in hiding for the Thief to return. The Thief is an Acolyte. At the end the Acolyte breaks another huge branch off while he is dancing and runs off. The Garden Owner and his Friends chase out after the Acolyte.

HANA ORI 花折 (Forbidden Blossoms)   I O 和 大

Shite	ACOLYTE
Ado	HEAD PRIEST
Koado	HEAD FLOWER VIEWER
Tachishū	GROUP OF FLOWER VIEWERS

The Head Priest goes out on some business, and leaves the Acolyte to watch the place ordering him not to let anyone in to see the flowers in the temple grounds. The Head Priest leaves, and the Acolyte closes the doors.

The Head Flower Viewer gathers his friends and they

proceed to the temple with provisions for a drinking party under the blossoming trees. They reach the temple, and try to convince the Acolyte to let them in. He refuses, so they decide to begin their party outside since they can see the flowers from this position anyway.

The Acolyte hears their noisy party, goes out, and tells them that they must leave the area. The Flower Viewers say that they are on free land over which the temple has no jurisdiction. The Acolyte says that since they are viewing the temple's flowers, they should at least give an offering of *saké* to the flowers.

The Flower Viewers decide to get the Acolyte drunk and trick him into letting them inside the temple grounds. The Head Flower Viewer gives the Acolyte several cups of sake and finally persuades him to let only him inside the gate. When the gate is opened, they all rush in. The Acolyte joins them without much objection and they begin their party inside. All enjoy themselves thoroughly, dancing, singing, and drinking.

The Flower Viewers decide to go home since it has begun to get dark, and the Acolyte, who is now quite drunk, presents each of them a branch of blossoms, then goes off to sleep on the floor.

The Head Priest comes home, finds the doors open, the branches all broken and the flowers mostly gone, and finally the Acolyte on the floor. The Acolyte, still drunk, says as he awakens, "If you want more flowers, I will break off as many branches as you want." The Acolyte realizes suddenly who he is talking to, begs for forgiveness, and is chased off by the Head Priest who is in a rage.

HANATORIZUMŌ　鼻取相撲
(Nose-Pulling Sumō)

Shite　DAIMYŌ
Ado　TARŌ KAJA
Koado　MAN FROM BANDŌKATA

A Daimyō orders Tarō Kaja to go out and find someone to hire as a new servant. Tarō Kaja finds a Man from Bandōkata and brings him to meet the Daimyō. When asked what he does best, the Man says he is good at *sumō* wrestling. The Daimyō is happy to hear this because he too likes *sumō*, so he asks for a demonstration. There is no one to wrestle with him, so the Daimyō finally agrees to be the other wrestler.

The Man twists the Daimyō's nose and wins the first round. When asked what kind of *sumō* this is, the Man answers it is a form popular in his home town called Nose-Pulling *Sumō*.

The Daimyō puts on earthenware nose-protectors and challenges the Man again. This time the Daimyō wins and the Man challenges him a third time. The Man wins this time, thus becoming champion, and leaves.

The Daimyō angrily takes off his nose-protectors and throws them away. Unwilling to admit defeat, he throws Tarō Kaja, who has had absolutely no experience at *sumō*, and goes off shouting, "I've won! I've won!"

HARA TATEZU　腹不立
(Priest Angerless Honesty)
(Ōkura title written: 腹立てず)

Shite　PRIEST

85

Ado   MAN I

Koado   MAN II

Two men who have just built a shrine near their homes in the country go out together in search of a priest to take care of and perform the ceremonies for their shrine.

A Priest who has only recently taken his vows comes along soon. They ask him where he is going and he replies he is like a leaf in the wind, he goes whichever way the wind blows. They hire him and start off toward home. They ask him about his skills and he brags about his talents. When they ask him about his name, he quickly makes up the name Hara Tatezu no Shōjiki-Bō which means "Priest Angerless Honesty," and he says the reason he was given this name is because he has never told a lie and has never gotten angry.

The two Men get a little fed up with his bragging. They decide to tease him and see if they can make him angry. They make several puns on his name, but he does his best not to show his anger. Finally he bursts into tears. They begin to beat him, but he gets away and runs off crying. They follow him off shouting, "Fake! Fake!"

HARIDAKO 張蛸 (Dried Octopus)

I

和

Shite   WEALTHY MAN

Ado   TARŌ KAJA

Koado   SELLER OF DRUMS

A Wealthy Man sends his servant Tarō Kaja to the capital to buy a dried octopus. Tarō Kaja doesn't know the meaning of the word *haridako*, so when he reaches the capital he begins shouting that he wants to buy one. A dishonest Drum Seller decides to trick Tarō Kaja into buying a drum which is called *haridaiko*. He tells Tarō Kaja that the thick skin which the Master has ordered is the head of the drum which produces a beautiful sound because it is thick, the bent wood ordered is the body of the drum, and the warts of the order are the nail heads seen around the drum head.

Tarō Kaja pays an enormous sum for the drum, takes it home and explains why he bought it. The Master gets angry and chases him out. The dishonest Drum Seller taught Tarō Kaja a song as a special service which he now begins to sing and dance in order to soothe his Master's anger. The Master hears the song, comes out to dance with Tarō Kaja and rewards him for his clever song.

HIGE YAGURA 髭櫓
(The Fortified Beard)

			和 大

Shite	MAN WITH A BEARD
Ado	WIFE
Koado	MESSENGER
Tachishū	NEIGHBORHOOD WOMEN

A Man who has a long thick beard has been chosen to carry the ceremonial halberd in the harvest festival because of his beard of which he is very proud. He calls his Wife to tell her the news, but she is not the least bit happy, especially when she hears that they will have to buy a special costume for the occasion. He orders her to comb and clean his beard and she not only refuses, but begins to insist that he shave it off. This leads to a full-fledged argument. She goes off in tears.

A Messenger comes to warn the Man that his Wife has gathered all the Women in the neighborhood and they are coming, with various weapons including a huge pair of tweezers, to pull his beard out by the roots. The Man fortifies his beard with a turret-like scaffold, thus preparing himself for battle. The Women arrive led by the Wife, and a noisy fight ensues. The Wife breaks through the fortification and pulls the beard out by its roots. The Man is left beardless and sad.

HIKKUKURI 引括 (Tied Up in a Sack)　　I
　　　　　　　　　　　　　　　　　　　　　　　　　和

| Shite | MAN |
| Ado | HIS WIFE |

A Man and his Wife have been married for five or six years. She is so ill-tempered that he can't take it any longer, so he decides to divorce her and send her home to her parents. He knows she will give him a hard time, so he begins by saying that since she has worked so hard and faithfully these five years, he wants to give her a little vacation to go visit her parents. She says she doesn't want to see her parents, and besides if she took a vacation it would be just that much more work to catch up on when she came back. He tries to convince her, but she is adamant. Finally what started as a seemingly pleasant conversation turns into a quarrel. She finally says, "If you want to divorce me, just say so like a man!" He retorts, "All right! I want a divorce! Get out!" She says she will but she wants to take a few things with her. He says to take whatever and however much she likes. She brings out a sack and asks if she can take this sackful. He says, "Take as many sackfuls as you like." She makes him promise he will not object to anything she chooses. He agrees as long as she will take it and go as quickly as possible. She throws the sack over his head and pulls it tight saying, "This is what I want." She drags him off screaming to be released.

HIKUZU 籾屑 (Tea Chaff)

I
和

Shite	TARŌ KAJA
Ado	MASTER
Koado	JIRŌ KAJA

The Master calls Tarō Kaja and explains that the day of the dedication of Uji Bridge is near, and since it is also the memorial day for his ancestors, he must prepare something for the guests. He decides that all they will need is something to quench their thirst, so he decides to use the chaff from the worst tea he has to make the drink. He orders Tarō Kaja to grind the tea while he goes out on some business or other. Tarō Kaja objects that he has other work to do, and suggests the job be given to Jirō Kaja. The Master reminds him that just that morning he had objected to going on an errand and that Jirō Kaja had been sent in his place and has not returned yet.

Tarō Kaja agrees and starts to work soon after the Master has gone out. He soon dozes over his work. Jirō Kaja returns home, wakes him up and tries to keep him awake by telling him about a *sumō* match, then by doing a dance, but nothing seems to have any effect on the sleepy Tarō Kaja. Finally

Jirō Kaja gives up and decides to tease him a little by putting a demon mask on his face.

The Master comes home, is frightened out of his wits, and calls Jirō Kaja to chase the demon out. Tarō Kaja finally convinces them that it is really him and that he was somehow changed into this form while he was taking a nap, but the Master still wants nothing to do with a demon, no matter who it was before. Jirō Kaja assures the Master that he will take care of things and has him go into the house.

Jirō Kaja proceeds to throw Tarō Kaja out, and in the struggle which ensues, the mask comes off. Jirō Kaja admits it was he who put the mask on Tarō Kaja, and Tarō Kaja chases him off cursing.

HI NO SAKÉ 樋の酒 (Piped In Saké)

I

和

Shite	TARŌ KAJA
Ado	MASTER
Koado	JIRŌ KAJA

The Master calls Tarō Kaja and Jirō Kaja, and tells them he must go out on some business or other. He leaves Tarō Kaja in charge of the rice storehouse and Jirō Kaja in charge of the saké storehouse ordering them not to leave their posts.

They get bored and begin chatting through the windows which face each other. The saké smells so good that Jirō Kaja decides to taste some and invites Tarō Kaja to come join him. Tarō Kaja very conscientiously says he must stay at his post, so Jirō Kaja feeds him saké through a large bamboo pipe which he puts across between the two windows.

They both get quite drunk and are enjoying themselves singing and dancing when the Master comes home and chases them out scolding.

HISSHIKI MUKO 引敷聟

(The Groom with a Leather Loin Cloth)

I
和

Shite	GROOM
Ado	FATHER-IN-LAW
Koado	TARŌ KAJA
Koado	FRIEND (OF GROOM)

A Groom is trying to get ready to make his ceremonial first visit to his Father-in-law, but he doesn't have the proper clothes. He has been able to borrow everything but the lower outer garment called a *hakama*. He goes to borrow a *hakama* from a Friend, but the Friend only has an extra upper outer garment. They tie the upper garment on the Groom to look like a *hakama*, but since this only covers the front, the Friend also loans him a leather loin cloth (a garment used when hunting to protect the seat of the *kimono*). The Friend advises him not to take this loin cloth off under any circumstances.

The Groom proceeds to his Father-in-law's house and when asked about the loin cloth, he says he has just come in from hunting. The Father-in-law insists that he take the loin cloth off, the Groom objects, and Tarō Kaja pulls it off of him. Even so the ceremony goes along smoothly till the Father-in-law insists that the Groom dance for him. The Groom gets out of this fix by dancing facing the Father-in-law, but then the Father-in-law insists on dancing together, during which he discovers the back of the *hakama* is missing. The Father-in-law begins to laugh and the Groom runs off embarrassed. The Father-in-law hurries off after him saying, "Never mind. Don't worry about a little thing like that!"

HITO O UMA 人を馬 (Man Into Horse)

I
和

Shite	DAIMYŌ
Ado	TARŌ KAJA
Koado	MAN FROM BANDŌKATA

A Daimyō orders Tarō Kaja to go out and find someone to hire as a new servant. Tarō Kaja finds a Man from Bandōkata and brings him to meet the Daimyō. When asked what he can do, the Man says the reason he left home was because there is nothing special he can do. The Daimyō says he can't use anyone without any skills or talents. Tarō Kaja pleads for the Man, but to no avail.

The Man wants the job very badly and finally says that there is one thing he can do, he can change a man into a horse. The Daimyō asks him to demonstrate to which the Man responds he must have someone to demonstrate on.

The Daimyō orders Tarō Kaja to be the victim, but Tarō Kaja strongly objects. The Daimyō threatens to kill Tarō Kaja, and Tarō Kaja finally agrees.

The Man takes Tarō Kaja aside and explains he has never made a man into a horse before so they will just have to pretend. Tarō Kaja puts on the bridle and bit, gets down on all fours, paws the ground, and makes noises like a horse.

The Daimyō is so impressed that he gives the Man his sword,

but on closer inspection realizes that the "horse" still looks like Tarō Kaja. The Man tries to explain that it takes time for the actual transformation of the body to take place. The Daimyō realizes he has been tricked when he tries to ride the "horse." He beats Tarō Kaja and chases them both off demanding his sword back.

HŌCHŌ MUKO 庖丁聟
(The Butcherknife Groom)

Shite	GROOM
Ado	FATHER-IN-LAW
Koado	WIFE (OF GROOM)
Koado	TARŌ KAJA
Koado	FRIEND

A Groom in preparation to make his ceremonial first visit to his Father-in-law's house goes to ask a Friend about the proper procedure for the ceremony. The Friend decides to tease him a little and gives him a list of instructions which he says will tell him all he needs to know.

The Groom cannot read, so he takes his Wife along to read the instructions at the proper time. They arrive at the Father-in-law's house and everything goes well until the Groom decides it is time to perform the ceremony as written in the document.

The Wife begins to read and the Groom follows the instructions which are actually for *sumō* wrestling. The Father-in-law realizes what has happened and decides to go along with the joke so as not to embarrass his new son-in-law.

They begin to wrestle, the Wife tries to join in, but has

93

trouble deciding which one to help. Finally she joins forces with the Groom. They throw the Father-in-law and go off happily together. The Father-in-law gets up, brushes himself off and calls out after them, "This is a fine way to treat your Father-in-law! Just for that, I'll never invite you to the festival again!"

Notice that the title has no relationship to the story. There seems to be no good explanation for this.

HŌJŌ NO TANE　謀生種
(The Tall Tale Seed)

Shite	NEPHEW
Ado	UNCLE

A Nephew, whose Uncle is a great teller of tall tales, has spent some time trying to think up a story taller than his Uncle can tell. He has finally thought of a story he thinks will do the trick and goes to visit his Uncle.

He begins by telling his Uncle that he went on a pilgrimage to Mount Fuji. The Uncle is, of course, anxious to hear about his trip.

The Nephew says that one night in a camp at the foot of Mount Fuji, a young man began bragging that he could put a paper bag over Mount Fuji. Everyone, of course, thought he was crazy and bet him he couldn't do it. With the help of his friends, he gathered all the paper available in the surrounding area, made paste from rice, and beginning from the bottom of the mountain pasted pieces of paper together, so that by the time he reached the top, the whole mountain was covered with one huge paper bag.

94

The Uncle agrees that this is an unusual story, but says that he saw an even more amazing thing happen the previous year when he went to Kōshū. One evening when he stayed on the shores of Lake Biwa, he saw some men make the lake into tea and drink it dry. They did this by collecting all the tea in the area, pouring it into the lake, then after stirring it with a tea whisk fifty-four meters long, they blew off the foam and drank it. The foam formed what is now known as the Awazu-ga-hara Plain.

The Nephew objects that the Plain was already in existence at the time of the Genji and Heike Wars. The Uncle claims that the one he is refering to is called the New Awazu-ga-hara Plain.

The Nephew laughs at his Uncle's attempt to cover up his mistake and says that recently he saw a cow lying in the Innami Plain while eating the grass off Awaji Island. The Uncle asks, "How can that be? The Innami Plain and Awaji Island are separated by a river, a mountain, and the ocean." The Nephew answers, "It was a very big cow."

The Uncle says that when he went to the Kantō Plains, he saw a drum that was four miles in diameter. The Nephew says, "Don't be ridiculous! Where in the world did they find a skin big enough for a drum that size?" The Uncle answers, "They took it off the cow you saw."

At this the Nephew is so put down that he gives up and admits what he was trying to do. The Uncle pretends to enjoy the joke and tells the Nephew that he has some Tall Tale Seeds that he has never even told anyone about before, but since he is such a good sport he will let him have one. However, he must dig it up for himself.

The Nephew is very pleased and digs here and there in several places his Uncle says there should be seeds. He soon realizes that he has been taken in again and chases his Uncle off.

HONE KAWA 骨皮 I O
(The Mixed-up Acolyte) 和 大

Shite	ACOLYTE
Ado	HEAD PRIEST
Koado	MAN I
Third Ado	MAN II
Fourth Ado	MAN III

The Head Priest calls the Acolyte and informs him that beginning today he will be the new head priest. The Head Priest himself will retire, but will stay in the temple and will be happy to give advice at any time. The Acolyte is very happy about his promotion, and is very anxious to make a good impression.

Before long a Man comes asking to borrow an umbrella. The Acolyte loans him the best umbrella in the temple. He goes to tell the Head Priest what he has done, expecting to be praised, but instead is scolded. The Head Priest tells him that next time someone comes borrowing such things, he should tell them that the old priest had taken it out in the rain, and it was blown to pieces, the skin torn from the bones, so that they tied it together and hung it up in the loft, therefore it is now quite useless.

Next a Man comes asking to borrow a horse to which the Acolyte replies exactly as he has been told. That is, the horse was taken out in the rain where it was blown to pieces by the wind, skin from bones, so they tied it together and strung it

96

up in the loft. The Acolyte tells the Head Priest what he has done and this time he is told that he should have said that they had put it out to pasture where it went crazy and lost the use of its legs, so they tied it in the corner of the stable.

Next a Man comes asking the Acolyte and the Head Priest to come to dinner at his house the next day. The Acolyte replies that he will gladly accept the invitation, but that the old Head Priest was put out to pasture where he went crazy and lost the use of his legs, so they tied him in the corner of the stable.

He again goes to tell the Head Priest what he has done. The Head Priest gets very angry, throws him down, beats him, and chases him off.

In the Ōkura script, the Acolyte gets angry at the end, throws the Head Pricst down and runs off. The Head Priest picks himself up and yells out after the Acolyte, "Treating your elders like this will give you an unhappy future!"

HŌSHI GA HAHA 法師が母
(The Baby's Mother)

I O
和 大

Shite   DRUNKARD
Ado   WOMAN (DRUNKARD'S WIFE)

A Man comes home drunk, fights with his Wife and throws her out. Later when he sobers up and the baby begins crying for its Mother, he goes out searching for his Wife, finds her, apologizes, and they return home happily together. The search, meeting, apology and return home are all done in song and dance.

IGUI 井杭 (Igui, the Disappearing Boy) 　　I O

(Ōkura title written：居杭 　　　　　　　　　　和 大

Shite	IGUI
Ado	MAN (FRIEND OF IGUI)
Koado	FORTUNE TELLER

A young boy named Igui is in the habit of visiting a Man's house where they treat him very well except for the fact that everyone pats him on the head. He doesn't like being patted on the head, so he goes to a shrine and prays for some solution for his problem. He is presented with a cap and told to put it on whenever someone pats him on the head.

Igui goes to visit the Man and sure enough gets patted on the head. He puts the cap on, and finds he is invisible. He is enjoying himself appearing and disappearing when the Man

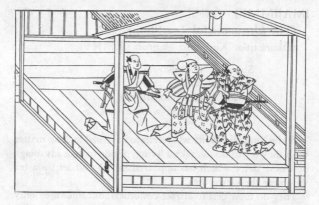

calls in a Fortune Teller to help him find Igui who has stayed invisible for some time.

The Fortune Teller is quite skillful and is able to tell exactly where Igui is, but when they try to catch him, he always moves. Finally the Man loses faith in the Fortune Teller and begins to get angry.

Next Igui steals the Fortune Teller's equipment, and throws it at the two a piece at a time making them more and more irritated. Then he begins pinching their noses and pulling their ears. They, of course, accuse each other of these things, really get angry and start to fight. Igui sees that the fun is over, takes off his cap and says, "Here I am! See if you can catch me!" He takes off at a dead run, and the Man and the Fortune Teller join forces and chase out after him.

IMAJIMMEI 今神明
I O
和 大
(The Unsuccessful Tea Shop)
(Ōkura title: Kurikuma Shinmei 栗隈神明

Shite	HUSBAND
Ado	WIFE
Koado	FIRST WORSHIPPER
Tachishū	SEVERAL WORSHIPPERS

A Husband and Wife, who seem to have bad luck no matter what they try to do to make a living, decide to take advantage of a new deity which has appeared in Uji and set up a tea shop near the sacred area.

They do their best to attract customers, but since they only have one tea cup the tea is always dirty, since they don't have a big enough burner they can't keep the tea hot enough, since their tea is poor, and the Wife is much too ugly to attract customers, they fail once more in their attempt to make a living.

They break their utensils, throw them away, and start toward home singing sadly about their poor state of affairs.

In the Ōkura script, at the end the Man throws his Wife down complaining about her inability to attract customers. She gets up, picks up a stick, and chases him off.

IMA MAIRI 今参
I O
和 大
(Hired for a Riddle)

Shite	DAIMYŌ
Ado	TARŌ KAJA
Koado	IMA MAIRI

A Daimyō calls his servant Tarō Kaja and says he wants to hire more servants. Tarō Kaja asks how many, and the Daimyō says eight thousand. Tarō Kaja says that's too many. The Daimyō says two hundred and Tarō Kaja still objects. The Daimyō says one and sends Tarō Kaja out to the highway to look for a talented man to hire.

Tarō Kaja soon finds a Man and since the Daimyō is fond of *shūku* (a kind of double entendre riddle), Tarō Kaja teaches the new Man a few on the way home, but in the interview with the Daimyō, he forgets and gets them all mixed up. The Daimyō gets angry, so Ima Mairi (the new servant) explains that in his home town they do riddles to a rhythm, and if the Daimyō will try this method, he is sure he will do much better. The Daimyō agrees, they do several riddles this way, and finally begin a kind of dance. The new Man is hired and everyone is happy.

I MONJI 伊文字 (The Letter I)

I O
和 大

Shite	TRAVELLER
Ado	DAIMYŌ
Koado	TARŌ KAJA
Koado	WOMAN

A Daimyō takes his servant Tarō Kaja and goes to the Kiyomizu Temple to pray for a wife. They reach the temple, pray, then sleep. The Daimyō receives a message in a dream that the Wife he has prayed for is waiting for him at the Western Gate. The Daimyō sends Tarō Kaja who goes and finds her there. She quickly recites a poem in which she says she is from the land of Ise, the town of Ise Teramoto, then she disappears.

Tarō Kaja can't remember the name of the place. The Woman's poem had started with, "If you love me, come to my hometown for me, I . . ." The Daimyō and Tarō Kaja

decide to stop people to discover the rest of the poem, so they hold a rope across the road and wait.

A Traveller comes along who is in a great hurry, but they stop him, and tell him their problem. He doesn't want to cooperate, but they force him to. After a rather long discussion done in rhythm, he is finally able to help them find the correct answer. By the time they have finished, the sun is ready to set. They go off singing together.

INABADŌ　因幡堂
(A Bad Wife is Like a Bad Penny)

因 幡 堂

Shite	MAN
Ado	WIFE

A Man has just divorced his Wife because she is not only ill-tempered and doesn't do any of her housework, but is also an incurable drunkard. He had tried to divorce her before, but couldn't get her to leave. Finally she went to visit her parents, and he sent a letter after her declaring the divorce. Now that he has gotten rid of her, he goes to the Inabadō Temple to pray for a new wife.

In the meantime, the Wife has received the letter, and heard about his new plan. She goes to the temple in a rage and finds him sleeping there. She pretends to be the messenger and tells him that he will find his new wife on the steps of the Western Gate.

He finds his new Wife veiled at the Western Gate, takes her hand, and starts toward home. On the way he explains the situation to her, telling her all the bad points of his previous Wife and asks her to be a better wife. She seems to agree.

103

They get home, and he asks her to take off her veil. She refuses, so he suggests she is probably shy, so perhaps they should have a drink first. She happily agrees to this and once she starts drinking, she continues to ask for more and more. He finally gets her to stop and again asks her to unveil. She still refuses, so he takes her veil off himself. He is surprised. She is angry and chases him off scolding at the top of her lungs.

INU YAMABUSHI 犬山伏
(The Dog and the Yamabushi)

Shite	YAMABUSHI
Ado	PRIEST
Koado	TEA SHOP OWNER
Third Ado	DOG

A Shintō Priest stops by the Tea Shop of a friend of his on the way home. That morning when he went out it had looked like rain, but later the sun came out and he is tired of carrying his umbrella, so he asks if he can leave it with the Tea Shop Owner. The Tea Shop Owner agrees and they are drinking tea and chatting pleasantly when a Yamabushi comes storming in, orders tea, and complains first that it is too hot, then that it is too cool. He notices the Priest, pushes him off his stool, and sits on it himself. They begin insulting each other till the Priest gets frightened and tries to run away through the back door to which the Tea Shop Owner objects saying that he would be in trouble, because the Yamabushi has been insisting that the Priest carry his luggage.

The Tea Shop Owner says that he has a ferocious dog and

that they should settle their argument by seeing whose prayers have the strength to quiet the dog. He tells the Priest, who is deathly afraid of dogs, that if he uses the word Tora, which is the name of the dog, in his prayers, it will quiet down immediately. They agree that if the Yamabushi wins, the Priest will have to carry his luggage, and if the Priest wins, the Yamabushi will have to carry his umbrella.

The Priest prays first using the word Tora many times and the dog quiets immediately. The Yamabushi then tries every prayer and charm he knows but the dog only bites him for his trouble and finally chases him off. The Priest runs after them shouting, "I've won! You must carry my umbrella!"

IORI NO UME　庵の梅　　　　　　　　　I　O
(The Plum Blossom Hut)　　　　　　　和　大

Shite	NUN
Ado	WOMAN

105

It is early spring and a group of young women come singing to the hermitage of an aged Nun to view the plum blossoms. The hermitage is a hut made of live plum trees famous for their blossoms.

The Nun apologizes because the trees are the same age she is so that the blossoms are not as plentiful and beautiful as they used to be.

The Women offer the Nun *saké*. They all begin drinking, singing and dancing together. They finally convince the Nun to dance for them. Before she dances, she instructs them all to take branches of the blossoms as souvenirs, but says they must pick them themselves, for her arms are too old and weak to reach that high. The Women sing the accompaniment for the Nun's dance.

In the Ōkura script, the Nun is singing when the Women arrive and is embarrassed that they heard her. She has been expecting them because they come every spring at plum blossom time, so she is happy to see them. They have brought poem cards which they present to the Nun to read, then each one hangs her own on the branches of the tree. The party begins, and the rest of the play is the same as the Izumi script.

IROHA 伊呂波 (Learning the Alphabet)   I O
                                      和 大

Shite   SON
Ado   FATHER

A Father calls his Son and tells him he has reached the age

to go to school and before he starts, he should learn the alphabet. The Son wants to know why it is necessary to learn the alphabet and his Father responds, "In order to be able to distinguish between black and white." The Son says he learned that a long time ago, a crane is white and a crow is black. The Father explains that he was talking about paper and ink, in other words, the ability to read.

The Father says the whole alphabet in one breath, and the Son complains that when he says it like water running over a board, it is impossible to remember even one letter, so would he kindly teach it to him like an old man climbing a hill, one step at a time.

The Father tries to teach one letter at a time and the Son keeps coming up with things completely irrelevant. The Father sees he is getting nowhere fast, so he orders the Son to repeat after him. The Son not only repeats every word he says, but mimics every action, till the Father gets so exasperated that he throws his Son down. The Son, in turn, throws his Father Father down and runs off. The Father picks himself up and calls out after him, "You treat your Father this way, and you'll have bad luck in the future!"

IRUMAGAWA　入間川
(The Iruma River)

I O
和 大

Shite	DAIMYŌ
Ado	TARŌ KAJA
Koado	MAN FROM IRUMA

A Daimyō who has finished his business in the capital calls Tarō Kaja and they set out for home. Before long they reach

Suruga where they have a fine view of Mt. Fuji, and they stop for a time to admire it. Next they come to a wide river and wonder how to get across. Finally a Villager appears on the other side of the river and they question him. In answer to their questions, he replies that this is the Iruma River, the village is called Iruma, and the family name of the people is Iruma. Then he informs them that the river is deep at this point, so in order to cross, they must go upsream a short distance.

The Daimyō begins to cross immediately and gets completely drenched. He gets very angry at the Villager who can't understand this reaction because he had told the Daimyō that the water was deep in the immediate area. But the Daimyō says that he had heard that in the Iruma dialect, the opposite of the real meaning was always used. For instance, when a person says deep, he actually means shallow. The Villager says that not thinking the Daimyō would understand the local dialect, he had spoken in the standard dialect, but if the Daimyō wishes, he will speak in the Iruma dialect. This dialect consists mainly of the opposite use of positives and negatives which come at the very end of the sentence in Japanese.

The Daimyō enjoys hearing this upside-down language so much that he gives the Villager first his sword, next his dagger, then his fan, and finally, even the clothes he is wearing. Each time the Villager receives something he exclaims that he is not happy and not grateful. When the Daimyō has offered all he has, he says that now he would like to hear the truth. He asks the Villager to speak in the standard dialect and tell him truthfully whether or not he is happy and grateful for the gifts. The Villager replies that of course, he is happy, pleased and grateful.

108

The Daimyō, laughing, says that his request to speak the standard dialect was in Iruma dialect, thus meaning to continue to speak in the Iruma dialect, therefore the Villager's answer (according to the Iruma dialect) means that he is not grateful. If he is not grateful, he must not want the things, so the Daimyō grabs all the gifts and runs off with them.

ISHIGAMI 石神 (The Stone God)

I O
和 大

Shite	MAN (TARŌ)
Ado	FRIEND
Koado	WOMAN (WIFE OF TARŌ)

A Man goes to his Friend's house to ask for advice because his Wife has threatened to leave him on account of his drinking habits. The Friend says the only way to solve the problem is to promise to stop drinking. The Man gladly promises to do so.

The Woman comes also for advice. The Friend tries to convince her to reconsider, but she is adamant. The Friend then advises her to at least go to the temple at Izumo, and ask the Stone God for advice.

As soon as the Woman leaves, the Friend dresses the Man up as the Stone God, and sends him to the temple to make sure his Wife gets the correct advice.

The Woman arrives at the temple, and thinking she is praying to the Stone God, asks it to stand up if she should stay with her husband. The Stone God (actually the Man) immediately stands. The Woman decides to test it once more. This time she says if she should stay with her Husband, to

stay seated. The Man sits as motionless as a rock.

The Woman is disappointed, but since it is the will of the Stone God, she promises to go back to her Husband. She dances a ceremonial dance in thanks for the advice. The Man becomes interested in her dance, takes off the god-mask to see her better, and finally begins to dance with her. She discovers him, and chases him off scolding all the way.

IWAHASHI 岩橋 (The Shy Bride)

和

Shite	HUSBAND
Ado	GO-BETWEEN
Koado	WIFE

A new Husband goes to see the Go-Between to complain that he has been married ten days already, but his new Wife has neither spoken a word nor unveiled yet. The Go-Between

110

tells him that the Wife is a great lover of poetry, so if he will just recite a couple of poems, she will undoubtedly take off her veil and become friendly. The Go-Between trys to teach the Husband the poems, but he has a very poor memory. The Go-Between writes the poems on a piece of paper and gives them to the Husband, warning him not to let it be known he is reading the poems.

The Husband goes home happily. His Wife indicates that she will unveil if he recites some poetry, but she becomes shy again when the time comes. He forces the veil off, and almost passes out when he sees how ugly she is. He throws her down, and tries to run away, but she jumps up and runs out after him saying, "Don't run away! We will have many happy poetic years together!"

JISENSEKI 二千石
(Saved by a Resemblance)

I O
和 大

Shite	MASTER
Ado	TARŌ KAJA

Tarō Kaja took off work for a few days without his Master's permission and went to the capital. His Master heard that Tarō Kaja had come back the previous night, and goes to his house in a rage. He wants to do away with Tarō Kaja then and there, but first he wants to hear what he did and saw in the capital. Tarō Kaja says that singing and dancing are very popular, and offers to sing a song he learned especially to entertain his Master. When he sings, the Master becomes even angrier, because the song is one which has been treasured by his family for generations as a sort of family good luck charm.

The Master draws his sword ready to strike Tarō Kaja down, when he changes his mind saying that Tarō Kaja should not die without first hearing the story of the origin of this song. He tells the story in a long chanted narrative (*katari*). When he is finished and gets ready to kill Tarō Kaja, he bursts out crying. The Master asks him what he is crying about and Tarō Kaja answers that one time when the Master's father was still alive, he was asked to fetch a *shakuhachi* (a Japanese flute-like instrument). When he brought it he stumbled on something and fell, making the Master's father very angry. The father reached for his sword and threatened to kill Tarō Kaja. When the Master did the same just now, he looked and sounded so much like his father, that it made Tarō Kaja recall the days when the father had been alive, so that he couldn't help shedding tears.

At this the Master also begins to sob, and not only forgives Tarō Kaja, but gives him the sword. Tarō Kaja says that this quick change to kindness and this kind gesture are also just like the dead father. They cry together with tears of sadness for the departed and tears of happiness that the Master is so like his father. They finally dry their tears. The Master says that since his resemblance to his father is a sign of good luck, they should laugh together in celebration. Tarō Kaja agrees and is especially happy at having once again saved his own neck by using his head. They laugh heartily together.

JISHAKU 磁石 (The Human Magnet) I O
和 大

Shite HUMAN SELLER
Ado COUNTRY MAN (FROM MITSUKE)

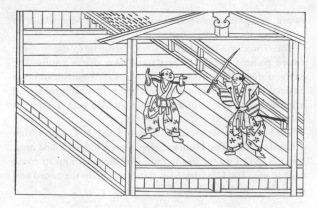

Koado   TEA SHOP OWNER

A Country Man comes to the capital to find a new home because he has had a fight and cannot return to his home town. A Seller of human beings offers to find him a job. The Seller takes the Country Man to a tea shop, and since he says he is sleepy, tells him to lie down and sleep because they will spend the night there.

The Human Seller, thinking the Country Man is asleep, sells him to the Tea Shop Owner who promises to pay him over the back fence at dawn, then he also lies down to sleep.

The Country Man, only pretending to be asleep, hears the whole conversation, and not only runs away, but receives the payment for himself over the back fence before he goes.

The Human Seller wakes up later, and sees the Country Man has escaped. He tries to get his pay anyway, but the Tea Shop Owner says he has already payed. The Human Seller realizes what has happened, borrows the Tea Shop Owner's sword, and goes out to search for the Country Man whom he soon runs into on the road.

The Country Man, thinking fast, threatens to swallow the sword pointed at him. When asked how that is possible, he explains that he is a Magnet from Magnet Mountain and that he drinks metal. The Human Seller begins to sheathe the sword in order not to lose it, and the Country Man begs him not to because he will die.

The Human Seller sheathes the sword and the Country Man pretends to die. The Human Seller regrets having killed him, lays the sword down beside him, and shouts at him to come back to life. The Country Man jumps up, grabs the sword and chases the Human Seller off.

JIZŌ MAI 地蔵舞   I O
(The Dance of the God Jizō)   和 大

Shite   PRIEST
Ado   INNKEEPER

A Priest arrives in a town towards evening, and finds a sign stating that it is against the law for the citizens of this town to put travellers up for the night. He ignores the sign and asks an Innkeeper for lodging for the night.

The Innkeeper refuses, referring to the law. The Priest then asks him to keep his straw hat for the night to which the Innkeeper agrees. Later the Priest sneaks into the house, puts his straw hat on his head, and sits down where it was, thus being directly under the straw hat.

The Innkeeper discovers him, and tries to chase him out, but the Priest explains that since the Innkeeper has promised

114

to keep the hat for the night, he shouldn't object to the Priest sitting under it since the amount of space used is still the same. This amuses the Innkeeper, so he invites the Priest not only to stay the night, though it is against the law, but also to drink with him. While they are drinking, the Innkeeper asks the Priest to sing and dance. The Priest responds with a song and dance about the god Jizō.

JŪKI 重喜 (Jūki, the Clumsy Acolyte)　　I　O
　和　大

Shite	ACOLYTE (JŪKI)
Ado	HEAD PRIEST
(Koado	WORSHIPPER, Ōkura only)

Jūki, a very clumsy acolyte, is called by the Head Priest. The Head Priest tells him that he must go out to perform a service, and will take Jūki along with him. Jūki is very happy, and says that since they are going out together, they will probably get a big donation. The Head Priest scolds him saying that money means nothing to priests like themselves.

"But," Jūki says, "when you get a big donation, you come back very happy. When you get a medium donation, you are medium happy, and when you get no donation at all, you are in a very bad mood, and take it out on poor innocent me." The Head Priest says that that all may be so, but still donations are things one doesn't speak about.

In preparation to go out, the Head Priest decides he needs his head shaved, and since there is no one else about, finally decides to have Jūki do it. Jūki brings the razor and approaches the Head Priest to begin his work. When he comes too close, the Head Priest scolds him saying that an acolyte should always keep a distance of at least seven feet between him and his master for fear of stepping on his master's shadow. Jūki says that he did not know this, and apologizes humbly.

Jūki gets a bamboo pole on which he attaches the razor, and begins singing while he shaves the Head Priest's head from a distance of seven feet. The Head Priest is pleased with Jūki's cleverness, and joins in the song until Jūki slips and slices off the end of the Head Priest's nose. Jūki gets out as fast as he can, and the Head Priest follows after, sadly lamenting the loss of the end of his nose.

In the Ōkura script, the Worshipper appears at the beginning to invite the Head Priest and Jūki to perform a service and have dinner at his house. Jūki informs the Head Priest and they begin preparations. The rest is the same as the Izumi script.

KACHIGURI 勝栗 (Dried Chestnuts)

I

和

Shite	FARMER FROM TSU
Ado	FARMER FROM YAMATO
Koado	TAX COLLECTOR

A Farmer from Yamato bringing persimmons and pears, and one from Tsu bringing rice cakes, potatoes, and dried chestnuts, come to the capital to pay their annual taxes. They meet on the road and decide to travel together. They pay their taxes and are asked to compose a poem each using the names of their own products. They each make a poem, are rewarded, and laugh so loud that they are ordered to compose an additional poem. Then one more poem is demanded of the Farmer from Tsu because he brought three different things. The Tax Collector serves *saké*, and the Farmers sing and dance in celebration.

KAGAMI OTOKO 鏡男
(The Man and the Mirror)

I O

和 大

Shite	MAN FROM ECHIGO
Ado	MIRROR SELLER
Koado	WIFE (OF SHITE)

A Man from Echigo has finished his business in the capital, and on his way home, he remembers that he had promised to take a souvenir back to his Wife. He stops by a market and the Mirror Seller sells him a mirror. He has never seen a mirror before, and is completely fascinated with it. He looks at his own face, tries several expressions, and decides that he must never get angry, because his face when he is angry frightens even himself. He thinks his Wife will be very pleased, because she will be able to make herself beautiful every day.

He reaches home. His Wife is very happy to see him. He gives her the mirror, and when she looks in it, she sees another woman. This makes her very angry, and no matter how he tries to explain, she will not believe that it is her own face she is seeing, since she also has never seen a mirror before. He takes it away from her saying if she doesn't appreciate it, he will give it to someone else. She chases him off scolding, still believing he has brought home another woman.

The Ōkura script begins after the Man has bought the mirror. The Mirror Seller does not appear. The rest is the same as the Izumi script.

KAGYŪ 蝸牛 (The Snail)　　　　　I　O
　　　　　　　　　　　　　　　　　　　　　　和　大

Shite	YAMABUSHI
Ado	MASTER
Koado	TARŌ KAJA

A Yamabushi gets tired and lies down in a thicket to rest.

The Master tells Tarō Kaja to go look for a snail to present to his grandfather as medicine for long life. Tarō Kaja objects that he has never seen a snail and doesn't know where to find one. The Master explains that they can be found in any thicket, that they are black on the top of the head, carry a shell on their backs, they sometimes show two horns, and are sometimes as big as human beings.

118

Tarō Kaja comes to the thicket where the Yamabushi is sleeping, wakes him up and asks him if he is a snail. The Yamabushi decides to have some fun with Tarō Kaja. He says he is a snail and proves it by showing his black headgear, his conch shell (carried at the waist by Yamabushi, and used as a horn to signal each other), and the decorations on his costume saying that these are his horns.

The Yamabushi reluctantly agrees to go with Tarō Kaja, but refuses to walk. He asks Tarō Kaja to carry him on his back, but Tarō Kaja says he is too weak. The Yamabushi then suggests they do a walking dance while singing an amusing song. They begin singing and dancing their way home.

The Master, worried because Tarō Kaja is taking so long to return, goes out to look for him, meets Tarō Kaja and the Yamabushi on the road, and thinks Tarō Kaja has lost his mind. Tarō Kaja explains while singing and dancing, and the Master tells him he has been tricked. The Yamabushi hides, jumps out and scares them, then goes on his way laughing at their stupidity. They chase after him grumbling about his cruelty.

KAICHŪ MUKO 懷中聟
(The Pocketed Groom)

和

Shite GROOM
Ado FATHER-IN-LAW
Koado TARŌ KAJA
Third Ado FRIEND (OF THE GROOM)

A new Groom on his way to his Father-in-law's house for his ceremonial first visit stops by to ask a Friend about the proper etiquette for this ceremony. The Friend teases him by giving wrong information. He says that it is very simple, all that is necessary is to put everything that the Father-in-law gives him into the breast of his kimono.

The ceremony progresses smoothly till the Father-in-law gives him a bow. He tries to follow the instructions, and finally succeeds in getting it into his kimono sideways, with the ends sticking out from both sleeves.

The Father-in-law decides to have a little more fun with him. He demands that the Groom dance. The Father-in-law enjoys the plight of the Groom who finally gets tired of being laughed at and leaves. The Father-in-law runs after him apologizing.

KAKI YAMABUSHI 柿山伏　　I O
(The Persimmon Thief)　　和 大

| Shite | YAMABUSHI |
| Ado | PERSIMMON OWNER |

A Yamabushi gets thirsty as he travels along, but there is nowhere to get a drink, so after making sure there is no one around, he climbs up a tree near the road to steal some persimmons.

The Owner comes along while the Yamabushi is still up in the tree. The Yamabushi hides among the branches, but can be clearly seen. The Owner decides to have some fun with him and says the thief in the tree is not a man, but a dog. If it is a dog, it will howl. The Yamabushi howls like a dog. The Owner looks again and says it's not a dog, but a monkey. If it's a monkey, it should scratch itself and chatter. The Yamabushi scratches himself and chatters like a monkey. The

Owner looks a third time, and says it's not a monkey, but a kite. If it is a kite, it should spread its wings and cry. The Yamabushi spreads out his fan and crys like a bird. The Owner says that after a kite spreads its wings and crys, it always flies away. The Yamabushi tries to fly, but instead simply falls from the tree and hurts his hip.

The Yamabushi demands that the Owner take care of him till his hip heals. The Owner refuses and the Yamabushi proceeds to pray him bad luck. The Owner, pretending to be affected by the prayer, staggers around and falls down at the Yamabushi's feet. The Yamabushi, gloating over his success, begins to order the Owner to do this and that. The Owner jumps up and chases him off cursing at his impudence.

In the Ōkura script, the Yamabushi is hungry when he first appears. At first the Owner says it is a crow, and forces the Yamabushi to caw like a crow. At the end the Owner starts off, the Yamabushi prays him back and orders him to carry him. The Owner pretends to give in and lets the Yamabushi get on his back. The Owner throws the Yamabushi down after he has gone only a few steps, and runs off. The Yamabushi picks himself up and calls out after the Owner, "Treat a holy man like this, and you will have a black future!"

KAKUSHIDANUKI 隠狸
(Hiding the Badger)

I
和

Shite   TARŌ KAJA
Ado   MASTER

The Master has heard that Tarō Kaja has been hunting badger lately. He has invited a friend over for badger stew, so he

121

calls Tarō Kaja, and asks him for one. Tarō Kaja claims he has never hunted badger in his life. The Master knows Tarō Kaja is lying, but says he must have heard wrong, and sends him to the market to buy a badger.

The truth is that Tarō Kaja had caught a big badger the previous night, and wants to sell it and make some money, so instead of going to buy one as he was told, he goes to sell the one he has caught.

The Master also has a plan. He knows that Tarō Kaja is a great *saké* drinker, and that the drunker he gets, the more honest he is. The Master sets out with a bottle of *saké* to find Tarō Kaja. He reaches the market place and before long Tarō Kaja appears, trying to sell his badger. When he sees his Master, he hides his badger behind his back, and pretends he was trying to buy, not sell.

The Master offers him a drink, which he refuses at first because of the place, but gives in, and is soon quite tipsy. The Master brings up the subject of badger hunting, and Tarō Kaja gives a detailed account of the best way to catch a badger. The Master asks him to dance after a few more drinks, and he dances and sings about a rabbit, skillfully hiding the badger throughout the dance.

The Master pretends to like the dance very much, and says he wants to learn it. He finally talks Tarō Kaja into dancing it together, so he can learn it, and while they are dancing, he grabs the badger. At the end of the dance, when the words of the song are, "It's a rabbit!", the Master responds with, "It's a badger!" Tarō Kaja looks surprised and says, "Where did that come from?" The Master answers, "From your belt!" Tarō Kaja cries, "I've been found out!" The Master chases him off scolding.

KAKUSUI 角水
(The Water Horn Groom)

Shite	GROOM FROM KŌICHI
Ado	RICH MAN
Koado	TARŌ KAJA
Koado	GROOM FROM TSU
Koado	GROOM FROM HARIMA
Koado	OTSU (DAUGHTER OF RICH MAN)

A Rich Man advertises that he will give his daughter Otsu in marriage to any skillful poet. A prospective Groom from Tsu, one from Harima, and one from Kōichi come to try their luck. The Rich Man gives the word "Water Horn" (*kakusui*) to use in the examination poem. They all three compose such good poems that the Rich Man cannot decide which to give the daughter to, so he has each of them look at her face one at a time, and says he will give her to the one who still wants to marry her after seeing her.

The Grooms from Tsu and Harima take to their heels as soon as they see her face. The Groom from Kōichi is the only one left (he hasn't seen her face yet), so the Rich Man says there is no need for him to look, that it is all settled.

Before the Groom from Kōichi realizes what has happened, he has promised to marry Otsu, and is left alone with her. She makes him promise they will live together happily the rest of their lives. He agrees, then asks to see her face. She is so ugly that he almost passes out, and says, "It doesn't matter how rich it may make me, I could never marry the likes of you!" He runs off, and Otsu chases off after him shouting, "What about your promise? Wait for me!"

123

KAMABARA 鎌腹

I O
和 大

(Unsuccessful Suicide with a Sickle)

Shite	TARŌ
Ado	WIFE (OF TARŌ)
Koado	ARBITER

Tarō and his Wife are in the heat of a most noisy quarrel. The Arbiter appears and tries to settle the fight. Both accuse each other of all sorts of laziness and uselessness. Finally Tarō takes his sickle, and says he is going to commit suicide by cutting his own stomach open for all to see what the ungrateful Wife has driven him to. She says, "Go ahead and cut yourself open, but no one is going to stay around to watch." She drags the Arbiter off and leaves Tarō there alone.

Tarō is in a real fix because his threat was only to put his Wife in her place. He had no intention of dying. Now there is nothing to be done but to die, so he tries to figure some way of dying that won't hurt. He tries to fall on the sickle, but he can feel the wound before his stomach touches the blade. He tries to stab himself, holding the sickle in both hands, but says the sickle refuses to come near his stomach. He ties the sickle to a tree, puts his arms around the tree and shoves his stomach against the sickle, but this time his stomach refuses to go near the sickle. He tries to run against the sickle from a distance, but this time his feet refuse to go all the way. He decides that his eyes are the problem, so he puts his hands over his eyes, but still fails.

Each time he calls for his Wife and the Arbiter and all his friends to come and watch, because this time he will die for sure. In the end, he decides the biggest problem is that there is no one around to watch him die. He decides to put off his suicide till another day when he has had time to think it over and plan it better. As for today, he decides to go to work. He asks a Passer-by to go tell his Wife he has given up suicide for today, so he is going to work and will be home at the regular time.

In the Ōkura script, the Arbiter talks Tarō into going to work as his Wife asked him to. Tarō agrees and starts off to work. On the way, he decides to commit suicide with his sickle because he is afraid that if his Wife gets angry again, she will murder him. He tries various suicide methods as in the Izumi script, but finally decides it is best to go to work and make up with his Wife that evening.

Just as he starts off to work, his Wife rushes on. She has heard he is trying to commit suicide, and has come to apologize and beg him to change his mind. He sees her coming, and pretends that he is determined to go through with the suicide. No matter how she pleads, he won't change his mind till she finally says, "Well, if you insist on dying, then give me a divorce first." He asks why, and she answers that she will jump in the river and die as soon as she receives the divorce. At this he finally agrees to give up his plan and accept her apology. She not only apologizes, but says she will do anything for him. He says, "In that case, commit suicide in place of me," and hands her the sickle. She grabs the sickle, begins screaming and stomping, and chases him off.

KAMINARI 神鳴 (Thunder)　　　　I O
(Ōkura title written: 雷　　　　　　和 大

| Shite | THUNDER |
| Ado | QUACK DOCTOR |

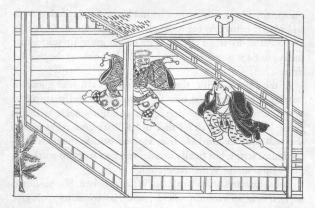

A Quack Doctor, on his way to Edo from the capital, comes to the Musashi Plains, and it begins to cloud over. Suddenly there is a loud noise, and Thunder stumbles through a hole in the clouds, and falls to the earth in the Doctor's path.

The Doctor is frightened out of his wits when Thunder demands his services. The Doctor examines him, and finds he has a cold and has hurt his hips in the fall. He administers cold medicine which Thunder complains is bitter, and acupuncture in both hips during which Thunder constantly complains about the pain. The Doctor assures him that even human beings can take this much pain.

Thunder gets up and prepares to leave. The Doctor demands his pay, and Thunder promises him good weather for the years to come for him and his relatives, then goes noisily on his way.

126

KANAOKA 金岡
(Kanaoka, the Love-crazed Painter)

Shite   ARTIST (KANAOKA)
Ado   WIFE (OF KANAOKA)

Kanaoka's Wife is worried about him because he hasn't been home for more than ten days. She has heard that he has lost his mind for some reason or other and is wandering around somewhere outside the city. She goes out to look for him, and when she reaches the Kiyomizu Temple, she decides to stop and rest there in hopes he will come by that way. Kanaoka has lost his mind over a girl, and is wandering around singing about his love and the cruelty of people who laugh at him as though he had actually gone crazy. He wanders to a spot near where his Wife is waiting, sinks to the ground, and begins crying to himself. The Wife sees him, goes over to him,

127

and asks what is wrong with him, and why he hasn't been home. He answers that there is nothing wrong with him, he is definitely not crazy, and to leave him alone. She says that one can see by just looking at him that something is definitely wrong, his clothes are in a mess, and his face is pale and sickly. He is surprised that it is so obvious, and says he will tell her the whole story if she promises not to get angry. She promises and he begins to tell his story.

Recently he was called to the castle near by to paint a picture on some doors. He painted a mural depicting the four seasons in which he put forth the best of his talents and knowledge. When it was finished, all the maids-of-honor and ladies-in-waiting insisted on seeing it, and among them there was one who was particularly beautiful. At this point, his Wife begins go get irritated, he reminds her of her promise which she renews, and he continues his story.

He tries to describe the girl's beauty by comparing her to the most beautiful things he can think of, but can think of nothing that even comes close. He was completely lost in admiration of her face, when she suddenly approached him, and asked him to paint something on her fan. He painted pictures on both sides, and gave it back to her. She smiled in thanks, and since that time, he has been able to think of nothing else but her lovely face when she smiled at him.

His story finished, he again breaks into tears. At this, his Wife flies into a rage. He says even though she promised not to get angry, and forced him to tell the story, she has, after all, gotten angry. She calms herself, and says that the reason that girl seemed so beautiful was because of her beautiful make-up, clothes, hair decorations, etc., and that if she were fixed up the same way, she would look just as attractive. Kanaoka says that with her black face, it wouldn't matter if one painted three days and three nights, she would still not look even presentable.

His Wife responds that since he is such a famous painter, he should be able to make her beautiful if anyone can, and begs him to at least try and see what happens. He finally consents, and paints a large red dot on each of her cheeks. He looks at her, then dances and sings that no matter how much paint one applies, a black mountain crow is still a black mountain crow, and that his Wife still doesn't in the least resemble his beloved.

This is the only Kyōgen in the whole repertoire that uses make-up.

KANAZU JIZŌ 金津地蔵
(The Impudent Jizō Statue)
(Ōkura title: Kanazu 金津

大
和
I O

Shite	CHILD
Ado	COUNTRY MAN
Koado	PARENT OF SHITE
Tachishū	GROUP OF FARMERS

A Country Man comes to the capital to buy an image of the Buddhist god Jizō for the new shrine he has built, but when he arrives, he remembers that he doesn't know where a sculptor lives, or what one looks like, so he decides to shout as he walks along the streets that he wants to find a Sculptor and buy a statue.

A dishonest Parent hears the Country Man and decides to trick him out of his money. He claims that he is the only true sculptor of a long line of famous sculptors.

The Country Man asks to see a sample and the Parent replies that he just happens to have a newly made one on hand, so if the Country Man will wait a minute, he will show it to him.

The Parent calls his own Child and explains what he has done. Since he has never carved so much as a tooth-pick, he asks the Child to cooperate in tricking the Country Man out of his money by becoming the statue himself. The Child is glad to do it to help his Parent since they are very poor, but is also sad to part with his family even for a short time. The Parent promises to go to the country and steal the Child back as soon as possible.

The Parent dresses the Child and takes him to show the Country Man explaining that he has just touched up the coloring a bit. The Country Man is surprised at its lifelike appearance, and even more surprised when he touches its face, and finds it warm. The Parent explains that it is warm because it is not yet dry.

The price is agreed upon, and the Country Man puts the Child on his back and prepares to leave. The Parent explains that the statue is so well made that it has a soul of its own, therefore it will always be warm, will require protection from the weather, and a little food now and then, and may even on occasion speak.

The Country Man goes on his way happily with his newly acquired treasure. He sets the statue up in the shrine when he reaches home, and calls all his friends and neighbors. They are very impressed with his purchase, and offer it incense and flowers.

The Child, who is the statue, thanks them for the offerings, but says he would be happier with some food. They bring the food, and he then orders *saké*. They decide to celebrate their good fortune in a song and a dance. Since the "statue" can speak and eat, they invite him to dance with them. All are dancing and singing merrily when the Child's Parent appears, takes the Child on his back and starts to leave.

The Farmers notice what has happened, and stop their dancing and singing. The Country Man who bought the "statue" recognizes the Parent, and all dash out in pursuit shouting, "Fake! Fake! Let's catch him."

In the Ōkura script, the Parent and the Country Man discuss specifications, then agree upon a time and place for the Country Man to pick up the statue the next day. The Country Man does not ask to see a sample. The Parent does not appear again.

The Country Men feed the "statue" and give him *saké* when he asks for it. The "statue" goes to sleep, and the Country Men wake him up and ask him to dance. All dance and sing in celebration of the living "statue."

KANE NO NE 鐘の音
(The Sound of Bells)

I O
和 大

Shite　　TARŌ KAJA
Ado　　　MASTER
(Koado　ARBITER Ōkura only)

The Master calls Tarō Kaja and sends him to Kamakura to ask the price of gold (*kane no ne*) because he wants to have a ceremonial sword made for his son who has just come of age.

Tarō Kaja misunderstands thinking the Master means the sound of bells (*kane no ne*—both "price of gold" and "sound of bells" are the same in spoken Japanese). He goes and listens to the bells of several temples and decides that the bell at

•Kenchōji is the best.

He goes home and reports to the Master who gets angry, explains what he really wanted, and chases Tarō Kaja out. Tarō Kaja makes up a song and dance about his mistake. The Master hears him singing, comes out to watch, and enjoys it so much that he forgives Tarō Kaja.

In the Ōkura script, the Master chases Tarō Kaja off trying to beat him. An Arbiter appears, asks what is wrong, and hears explanations from both sides. Tarō Kaja has the Arbiter apologize for him, and offers to sing the song about the temples and their bells. He sings and dances after which the Master scolds and forgives him.

KANI YAMABUSHI 蟹山伏   I O
(The Yamabushi and the Crab)   和 大

Shite   YAMABUSHI
Ado   ACOLYTE (SHITE'S SERVANT)

132

Koado   CRAB

A Yamabushi and an Acolyte, who is his servant, are on their way home after a period of study and meditation in which the Yamabushi has gained new powers and confidence. They talk about various things as they go along, the Yamabushi mainly bragging about his powers and his bravery.

Suddenly they hear a strange sound which frightens them both. They are wondering what it is when a strange form comes out of the forest by the road. They are both scared stiff, but finally the Yamabushi works up enough courage to go ask it what it is, and why it has appeared in this place.

The Creature answers that it is the spirit of an animal which has two eyes that look straight up, a shell that doesn't touch the ground, two big legs and eight small ones, and goes through life moving to the left and right. The Yamabushi realizes that it is the spirit of the Crab, and orders the Acolyte to break its shell with his stick. The Acolyte gets too close and gets

133

caught by the ear by one of its pinchers. The Yamabushi scolds him for being so clumsy, and proceeds to pray him loose.

The more the Yamabushi prays, the tighter the hold of the pincher becomes. Finally the Yamabushi gets too close too, and gets caught in the other pincher. The Crab throws them both down and disappears. They pick themselves up, and continue on their way somewhat less brave, and a great deal more humble than before.

KASEN 歌仙 (The Six Poets)

I

和

Shite	KAKIMOTO HITOMARU
Ado	WEALTHY MAN (DONOR OF PRAYER PLAQUE)
Koado	TARŌ KAJA
3rd Ado	JIRŌ KAJA
Poet	SŌJŌ HENJŌ
Poet	ARIWARA NARIHIRA
Poet	ONO KOMACHI
Poet	SARUMARU TAIYŪ
Poet	KIYOHARA MOTOSUKE

A Wealthy Man makes a pilgrimage to the shrine at Tamatsushima with his two servants Tarō Kaja and Jirō Kaja. The purpose of their pilgrimage is to donate a large prayer plaque dedicated to the six famous poets of the Heian Period.

They reach the shrine, hang up the prayer plaque, and pray. When they have finished praying, they notice that the pictures on the plaque seem to be coming to life.

The Six Poets appear, and begin joking among themselves and admiring the full moon. They decide to compose poems on subjects which they draw out of a hat. The subjects are rather difficult, so since it will take some time to compose their poems, they decide to begin drinking first. The first person who refuses a drink will be required to compose the first poem. Komachi pours the *saké* since she is the only woman present. She serves Shōjō first which makes all the others jealous.

When it comes Komachi's turn to drink, she refuses, so she has to recite her poem. Everyone criticizes her poem except Shōjō who praises it highly. The rest accuse Shōjō and Komachi of being in love at which Shōjō gets angry because he is a priest. He begins fighting with the others, and Komachi breaks up the fight. Shōjō rushes off followed by Komachi. He comes back on immediately with a halberd. There is a highly stylized fight accompanied by singing and poetry, until they hear the voice of the crow announcing dawn, at which they all scramble back to their places on the prayer plaque.

KAWAKAMI 川上   I
(Blindness, Sight, and Blindness Again)   和

| Shite | BLIND MAN |
| Ado | WIFE |

A Blind Man goes to pray to a miraculous statue of the Buddhist saint Jizō to give him back his eyesight. He spends the night at the temple. He chats with other people who have come to pray for various things, then goes to sleep, and receives a message in a dream that he will receive his eyesight if he promises to divorce his Wife. He is, of course, very happy, and promises to do as he is told.

His eyes open on his way home. His Wife comes out to meet him, and she is very happy to see that he has regained his eyesight, but very angry when she hears that she is going to be divorced. She finally convinces him that there will be no divorce, and that once the gods have given a man his eyesight, they are too compassionate to make him blind again no matter what he does after that.

They start back home together, and almost immediately, he becomes blind again. They both burst into tears. The Wife apologizes for her selfishness and promises to take care of him as she had done before. When his eyes were opened he threw away his cane, and now he wishes he hadn't been so hasty. She offers her hand to lead him, and they go off singing sadly, resigned to their fate.

KAWARA TARŌ 河原太郎 I O
(Tarō's Wife Revolts at Kawara) 和 大

    Shite   TARŌ
    Ado   WIFE
    Tachishū MANY VILLAGERS

Tarō's Wife takes the *saké* she has made to Kawara to sell it at the annual market. Tarō goes out after her to talk her out of a few sips. She refuses to give him even a drop till she sells some. He begs and pleads, but she is adamant. He finally gets so angry that he leaves saying he will beat her if she doesn't sell every drop of it.

Tarō waits on the road, stops everyone who comes by,

136

and tells them not to buy *saké* from his Wife because it is very poor this year.

The Wife hears what Tarō has done, and when he comes back later to see if she has sold any, she curses him up one side and down the other. He picks up a stick and begins beating her. She pretends to repent, and says she will serve him all the *saké* he wants. He drinks and drinks, and finally asks her to serve it to him "waterfall style," that is to pour it in the cup at such a rate that it is kept constantly full while he drinks. She pours the *saké* too fast, he complains, and she throws it in his face and begins cursing him again. Taro picks up the stick again and chases her off.

KAZUMŌ 蚊相撲 I O
(Wrestling with a Mosquito) 和 大

Shite	DAIMYŌ
Ado	TARŌ KAJA
Koado	MOSQUITO (NEW SERVANT)

A Daimyō sends Tarō Kaja out to find a new servant. Tarō Kaja meets a Man on the road, and brings him home. The new Man says he is good at *sumō* wrestling, so the Daimyō challenges him to a match. The new Servant is actually the Spirit of a Mosquito, and in the first round, he stings the Daimyō on the nose. The Daimyō thus discovers his true identity, so he brings out a huge fan, which he uses as a fly swatter, and wins the match.

In the Ōkura script, the Daimyō specifically orders Tarō Kaja to hire a *sumō* wrestler. In the latter part of the play, the Daimyō has Tarō Kaja use the fan, and he himself pulls the mosquito's stinger out, and wins the match. The Mosquito goes off buzzing sadly.

KEIMYŌ 鶏猫
(A Cat Killed for Killing a Chicken)

大 和
O I

Shite	SABURŌ
Ado	DAIMYŌ
Kokata	BOY (SON OF SABURŌ)
Koado	TARŌ KAJA
Koado	JIRŌ KAJA

A Daimyo's favorite Chinese cat has disappeared, and he puts up a notice stating that anyone giving information concerning the cat's whereabouts will be rewarded with anything he may ask for.

A Boy appears and reports that Saburō killed the cat. The Daimyō sends Tarō Kaja and Jirō Kaja out to capture Saburō.

They bring Saburō back, and when he sees the Boy, who is his son, he curses him as a traitor, and readily admits that he killed the cat and buried it in his field, because it had killed his favorite chicken. Since his Son has proved a traitor, he says, he is ready to die.

As they start to take Saburō off to execute him, the Boy stops them saying he hasn't yet received his reward. The Daimyō asks what he desires, and he answers that he wants his father's life spared. The Daimyō is reluctant, but finally agrees after the Boy tells him of a similar case which had taken place in China.

Saburō apologizes to his Son for having cursed him, and they start home together singing happily.

138

KEIRYŪ 鶏流
(Does a Cock Crow or Sing?)

Shite	TARŌ KAJA
Ado	MASTER

The Master orders Tarō Kaja to wake him when the cock "sings." Tarō Kaja oversleeps, so in order to get out of his predicament, he wakes his Master, and tells him it is already daylight, and that the cock has "crowed," but has not "sung" yet. The Master scolds him saying, of course he meant when the cock crowed. The Master goes on to explain that the reason he had used the word sing was because in classical poems, this is the word used. Tarō Kaja objects, giving several examples of old poems in which the word "crow" is used. The Master answers with one poem which uses "sing" reciting it in different ways claiming it may sound like the same poem but it was written by different authors. Finally he thinks of another poem the first line of which uses the word "sing," but Tarō Kaja reminds him that the second line uses "crow." The Master scolds him saying, "Can't you let your Master win an argument once in a while?"

KIKAZU ZATŌ 不聞座頭
(The Deaf Man and the Blind Man)

Shite	TARŌ KAJA
Ado	MASTER
Koado	KIKUICHI

The Master must go out on business, but is reluctant to

leave Tarō Kaja alone in charge of the house since he is deaf, so he calls Kikuichi, a Blind Man, to help Tarō Kaja out.

The two agree that if Kikuichi hears a burglar, he will tap Tarō Kaja on the knee. Nothing happens for some time and Kikuichi gets bored. He decides to tease Tarō Kaja, and taps him on the knee. Tarō Kaja begins calling for help and looking for the burglar. He sees Kikuichi laughing, realizes he has been tricked, and decides to pay Kikuichi back. Tarō Kaja tells Kikuichi that he has been taking dancing lessons and would like to dance for Kikuichi. Since Kikuichi is blind, Tarō Kaja promises to tap him on the shoulder to signal the end of his dance so Kikuichi can praise his efforts.

Tarō Kaja finishes his dance and taps Kikuichi on the shoulder, but with his foot (an extremely impolite thing to do in Japan), in answer to which Kikuichi praises him generously. Tarō Kaja laughs and laughs, and finally tells Kikuichi what he did.

Kikuichi, determined to get back at him, offers to sing a song, and since Tarō Kaja won't be able to hear it, he promises to raise his hand when he has finished. Kikuichi sings a song full of insults aimed at Tarō Kaja and his deafness. Tarō Kaja praises him, then Kikuichi laughs and tells him what the song was about.

Tarō Kaja, again out for revenge, offers to dance again for Kikuichi. Kikuichi warns Tarō Kaja not to tap his shoulder with his foot again, but when he finishes, he does just that. This time Kikuichi is ready for him. He grabs the foot and throws Tarō Kaja down, then begins searching for his cane. Tarō Kaja gets up, throws Kikuichi down, and runs off. Kikuichi shouts after him that he will have bad luck in the future for treating a poor innocent blind man this way.

140

KIKU NO HANA 菊の花   I O
(The Chrysanthemum)   和 大
(Ōkura title: Bōbōgashira 茫々頭

     Shite   TARŌ KAJA
     Ado   MASTER

Tarō Kaja took off work for a few days without his Master's permission, and went to the capital. His Master heard that he had come back the previous night and goes to his house in a rage. When he hears where Tarō Kaja has been, he says he will forgive him in return for a description of his adventures.

First Tarō Kaja tells about a sparrow and a crow that were on the same branch of a tree. The sparrow said, "Cheep, cheep," and the crow said, "Caw, caw," so Tarō is sure they were related. The Master doesn't think this the least bit interesting, so Tarō Kaja tells him how he was walking along a street, and saw some beautiful chrysanthemums. The owner gave him one, and since he felt strange carrying it, he stuck it in his hair. He soon met some beautiful girls who admired his flower by reciting a poem. He answered back with a poem, and they invited him to follow them. They came to the place they work which was a restaurant. He followed them in and sat down. He was moved to what he thought was a higher seat, because there were valuable things all around him, but his Master tells him it was the closet. Nobody paid any attention to him, so finally he got up and left. A beautiful girl came running out after him, and grabbed him by the ear. He showed her a diamond he had picked up in the closet, and gave it back to her. She let go of his ear, took the diamond, and went back to the restaurant.

His Master scolds him for his stupidity.

141

The Ōkura script is the same except that Tarō Kaja does not tell the first story about the sparrow and the crow.

KINTŌZAEMON　金藤左衛門
(*See* Yase Matsu)

KINYA　禁野
(Keep Quiet and Keep Out of Trouble)

Shite　DAIMYŌ
Ado　PASSER-BY

A Daimyō, on his way to hunt, stops a Passer-by who has been sent on urgent business, and forces him to accompany him. They reach Kinya, the place the Daimyō plans to hunt birds, and the Passer-by suddenly shouts that he sees a goose about

142

to take off. The Daimyō doesn't see it, so the Passer-by grabs the bow and arrow from him.

Instead of aiming at the goose, which was only a trick to distract the Daimyō's attention in the first place, the Passer-by aims at the Daimyō and demands his dagger and his clothes. He leaves the Daimyō shivering in his underwear.

The Daimyō tells a story in chanted narrative (katari) about a man who suggested that a human pillar was needed to complete a certain bridge, and, as a result, was used as the pillar himself. The man's daughter refused to speak from that day on. One day three years later the daughter was with a group in this very Kinya, when a pheasant cried out, and somebody shot it. The daughter spoke, reciting a poem, in which she said if it had kept its mouth shut it wouldn't have been shot. The people she was with asked her why she hadn't spoken for these three years, to which she replied that if her father had kept his mouth shut, he would still be alive.

The Daimyō goes sadly on his way mumbling that if he had kept his mouth shut, he would still have his clothes and his weapons.

KIROKUDA 木六駄 I O
(The Half Delivered Gift) 和 大

Shite	TARŌ KAJA
Ado	MASTER
Koado	TEA SHOP OWNER
Koado	UNCLE

It is the end of the year, and the Master orders Tarō Kaja to take six ox loads of firewood and six ox loads of charcoal plus a barrel of *saké* and a letter to his Uncle in the capital. Tarō Kaja objects that this is too much for one person to be responsible for, and besides it is much too cold to go out. The Master reminds him that there are no other servants in the house, and promises him especially warm clothes to wear.

When he reaches the mountain pass, it is snowing heavily, and he has a rather hard time herding the twelve oxen, keeping them in line, keeping their snow shoes on them, etc. He finally reaches the top with all twelve oxen. He stops at the tea shop on the top of the mountain to rest and get warm. Since he makes this trip every year, he has become friends with the Tea Shop Owner.

The Tea Shop Owner offers him tea, but he wants *saké*. The Owner apologizes saying that with all this snow, he hasn't been able to get any *saké* delivered, so he is out. Tarō Kaja is very disappointed. The Owner suggests that Tarō Kaja have a drink from the *saké* barrel he is carrying, and they can fill it up with water afterward. He at first objects, but is easily convinced.

Tarō Kaja drinks a few, then offers the Tea Shop Owner a drink. They begin to enjoy themselves drinking, singing, and dancing, till before they realize it, they have drunk all the *saké*. Tarō Kaja, now in high spirits, gives the empty barrel and the six ox loads of firewood to the Owner, and staggers on his way with the remaining six oxen.

He reaches the Uncle's house, and gives the Uncle the letter. When he is asked about the six oxen carrying firewood, he explains that he has changed his name to Kirokuda (meaning "six oxen carrying fire wood"), so the letter is referring to him. When asked about the *saké* he explains that it was so cold, that he drank it all at the tea shop on the mountain pass. The Uncle chases him off in a rage.

144

In the Ōkura script, the gift for the Uncle who lives not in the capital, but on the other side of the mountain, is only the barrel of *saké* and six oxen carrying poles to be used in building a new house. This is not a yearly gift, but is in celebration of the Uncle's new government position. The Master encourages Tarō Kaja to go by letting him drink plenty of *saké* before he starts on the trip.

The Uncle hasn't heard from his Nephew for a long time, so he decides to go see him. He stops at the tea shop on top of the mountain to rest and get warm. The Uncle is resting in an inner room when Tarō Kaja reaches the same tea shop.

The drinking party with the Tea Shop Owner and the gift of the six oxen carrying the poles is the same as the Izumi script. After the Tea Shop Owner receives the gift, he leaves Tarō Kaja and the Uncle in the tea shop. Tarō Kaja is by this time so drunk he doesn't know what is going on, and falls asleep on the floor.

The Uncle comes out, and finds Tarō Kaja asleep on the floor. He wakens Tarō Kaja, and Tarō Kaja gives him the letter. The rest is the same as the Izumi script.

KITSUNEZUKA 狐塚 (The Fox Mound)　I　O
和　大

(Ōkura titles: Kitsunezuka 狐塚 and Kitsunezuka Kouta Iri 狐塚小唄入

Shite	TARŌ KAJA
Ado	MASTER
Koado	JIRŌ KAJA

145

The Master sends Tarō Kaja out to his fields near the Fox Mound to scare away the birds by day and the wild animals by night.

Tarō Kaja scares several flocks of birds away during the day, but when the sun sets, he begins to get frightened when he hears strange sounds and sees fox fires. He is particularly afraid of being enchanted or changed into some other form by a fox. Foxes are known to roam about this area at night, and they try to fool people by assuming various shapes.

Jirō Kaja, and later the Master, come out to visit Tarō Kaja since they know he is afraid of the dark. He thinks they are foxes, catches and ties them up. Then he brings smoking branches, because smoke is supposed to force a fox to change back to his original shape. They, of course, only cough in the smoke, and finally imitate the cry of a fox so he will take away the smoke.

Tarō Kaja goes off to borrow a hoe with which to skin the foxes. While he is gone, the Master and Jirō Kaja help each other get loose, ambush Tarō Kaja, throw him down and run off. Tarō Kaja picks himself up and runs off yelling, "I'll catch you yet, you sly old foxes!"

In the Ōkura script, the Master sends Tarō Kaja and Jirō Kaja out together. Later he goes out to serve them *saké*. They think he is a fox changed into the form of their Master, so they detract his attention, and throw away each cup of *saké* he serves. Finally they catch him, and tie him up. He gets loose and chases them off. In the play called Kitsunezuka Kouta Iri (with song), Tarō Kaja and Jirō Kaja sing a song similar to the one in the Izumi script called Naruko before the Master comes out to visit them with *saké*.

KITSUNEZUKA KOUTA IRI 狐塚小唄入

(*See* Kitsunezuka)

KIYOMIZU ZATŌ 清水座頭   I

(The Blind Couple at Kiyomizu Temple)   和

Shite   BLIND MAN
Ado   BLIND WOMAN

A Blind Man and a Blind Woman both go to the Kiyomizu Temple to pray for someone to marry. They bump into each other, after which each discovers the other is blind. They apologize to each other, begin drinking and talking together, each sings a song, then they go to sleep.

The Blind Woman wakes up first, and has had a dream in which she received the message that her future husband would

147

pick her up at the Western Gate of the temple, so she goes there to wait.

The Blind Man wakes up, and he has also dreamed that he would find his future wife waiting at the Western Gate. He proceeds there to find her. They find each other, recognize the friend of the previous night, and go off singing happily together.

KOBU KAKI 昆布柿
(Seaweed and Persimmons)

和

I

Shite	FARMER FROM TANBA
Ado	FARMER FROM AWAJI
Koado	TAX COLLECTOR

A Farmer from Awaji brings persimmons, and one from Tanbe brings seaweed to pay their taxes. They meet on their way to the capital. They decide to travel together, reach the capital, and pay their taxes.

The Tax Collector asks their names. They have no names, so they make up nonsensical names for themselves. The first one says his name is "What shall I call myself," and the other makes up a very long name. The repeating of their names and the questions of the Tax Collector develop into a song. The Tax Collector says that it has been so pleasant that they should all three laugh together. They line up and laugh heartily.

148

KOBU URI 昆布売
(The Seaweed Seller)

Shite   SEAWEED SELLER
Ado   WELL-TO-DO MAN

A Well-to-do Man goes out alone, stops a Seaweed Seller, and forces him to carry his sword. The Seaweed Seller says that he must have both hands free to handle his seaweed, so the Man buys it all from him. He not only forces the Seaweed Seller to carry the sword, but teases him about the way he carries it, treats him as his own servant, etc., till he can't take it any longer.

The Seaweed Seller, using the Man's sword as a weapon, forces him to hand over his dagger, and then has him sell the seaweed, advertising it in very polite language, then in a song, then in a chant, then as a song and dance. The Man continues to demand the return of his sword and dagger the whole time. Finally the Seaweed Seller tires of teasing the Man and runs off with the sword and dagger with the Man in hot pursuit.

KOGARAKASA 小傘 (The Umbrella Sutra)

Shite   PRIEST
Ado   COUNTRY MAN
Koado   ACOLYTE
Third Ado   NUN
Tachishū   COUNTRY MEN

A Country Man has just built a small shrine, but has not yet hired a priest for it. He goes out to the highway to see if there might be a passing priest he can hire.

A Man has just lost all his worldly possessions gambling, and has decided to become a Priest and try to make a living in the country where no one will discover he isn't a real Priest. The new Priest goes to visit a friend of his, who is an Acolyte, before he leaves, to say good-bye and get some advice. They decide he can use a song about umbrellas, recited like a sutra, when he is asked to read a sutra or pray. The Priest remembers an old adage which says *sumō* is the shortest road to a quarrel, and gambling is the shortest road to becoming a thief. They agree that this is regrettable, but true. The Priest convinces the Acolyte to go with him, and they start out on their way together.

Before long they meet the Country Man on the road. He hires the Priest, and finally agrees to let the Acolyte come along too when the Priest assures the Country Man that he himself will accept all responsibility for the Acolyte who he says is his student.

They reach the shrine, and decide to have the opening ceremony immediately. The Country Man gathers all his friends, and they begin. The Priest tells them to leave their donations on the desk. They all give such things as swords, food, and an old Nun gives a *kimono*. The Priest begins the ceremony with a *nenbutsu* dance. Everyone begins dancing, and the Priest signals the Acolyte to take not only the donations, but also the sacred tools and books from the shrine. The Priest and the Acolyte take off with their loot.

When the people realize what has happened, they chase after the Priest shouting, "Fake! Thief!" The old Nun shouts, "Catch him! He has stolen the precious *kimono* I had planned to give to my grandchild." And she scurries after the Priest with the others.

KŌJI 柑子 I O
(Three Tangerines on a Branch) 和 大

Shite	TARŌ KAJA
Ado	MASTER

The previous night the Master had been given three tangerines growing on one branch at a party. Thinking this very unusual, he wanted to keep them, so he entrusted them to Tarō Kaja.

The Master calls Tarō Kaja to give him the branch. Tarō Kaja explains that he tied the branch on the end of his halberd, and as he was walking along, one of the tangerines dropped off, so he picked it up, peeled off the skin which was damaged, and ate it. Thinking he should take good care of the other two, he put the branch in the breast of his *kimono*. When he came through a crowded area, he was hit in the chest, felt a cool trickling sensation, and found that one of the remaining tangerines had been squashed, so in order not to lose any of the juice, he popped it into his mouth, and ate it whole.

The Master says it can't be helped as far as those two are concerned, and demands the remaining one. Tarō Kaja says there is a sad story about the remaining one, and recites a chanted narrative (*katari*) about Shunkan and his two companions who were exiled, the other two were pardoned and Shunkan was left alone.

The Master agrees that this is all very sad, but still wants the remaining tangerine. Tarō Kaja says that it looked so sad all alone that he ate it up too. The Master scolds him soundly.

KŌJIDAWARA 柑子俵
(The Tangerine Bag)

I
和

Shite	TANGERINE BUYER
Ado	TANGERINE GROWER
Koado	CHILD

A Tangerine Buyer has come to pick up his order for the
new year a little earlier than usual, therefore the Grower doesn't
have them packed in the straw bag yet. The Buyer says to pack
them, and he will be back that way to pick them up later.

Though the Tangerine Grower had already received the
Buyer's money for the tangerines, he has sold them to someone
else. He must put something or other in the bag to give to the
Buyer, so he calls his own Child, tells him the problem, and
asks him to get into the bag. The Child agrees. The Seller puts
a frightening devil mask on the Child, puts him in the bag, and
instructs him to take advantage of the first chance he has to run
away.

The Buyer comes back for his tangerines. The Grower helps
him put the sack on his back, and assures him that he has the
best tangerines in the country. The Buyer starts on his way
home, and getting tired before long, decides to put the sack
down for a while. He hears a voice saying, "Don't put it
down!" He look around, sees no one, and decides it was an
echo. He decides to hurry on his way when he hears a voice
say, "Don't hurry!" He realizes the voice is from the bag, and
gets frightened. He puts the bag down, and starts to run, but
the voice from the bag says, "If you don't open the bag, I'll

152

eat you alive." Trembling with fright, he opens the bag, sees the "devil" and takes to his heels, the devil chasing close behind.

KONO MI ARASOI　木実争
(The Battle of Fruits and Vegetables)

I O
和 大

Shite	EGG PLANT (ŌKURA: CHESTNUT)
Ado	TANGERINE
Tachishū	FRUITS
Tachishū	VEGETABLES AND NUTS

The Egg Plant and the Tangerine meet on the way to go flower-viewing on Mt. Yoshino. They decide to go together, but along the way their pleasant conversation develops into a quarrel, and finally the Tangerine beats the Egg Plant who runs off threatening to pay him back.

The other Fruits hear about the fight, and come armed to defend the Tangerine. The Egg Plant comes back with an army of Nuts and Vegetables. A violent battle is in full swing when suddenly a frosty wind blows which sends them all running for cover.

The Ōkura script begins with the Tangerine leading the other Fruits to the mountain for flower viewing. They are in the middle of a flower-viewing party, singing, dancing, and drinking, when the Chestnut comes storming in, demanding the reason for holding a party on his mountain without his permission. The Tangerine apologizes, and they invite the Chestnut to join them. He begins drinking with them, and the drunker he gets, the more he insults and makes fun of them, until they beat him and throw him out.

153

The Chestnut comes back with an army of Nuts and Vegetables. The rest is the same as the Izumi script.

KO NUSUBITO　子盗人
(The Amateur Kidnapper)

Shite	THIEF
Ado	NURSE
Koado	WEALTHY MAN

The Nurse has finally gotten the noisy baby to sleep, puts it to bed in an inner room, and relieved, goes back to get some other work done.

A Thief, who is not really a thief, but just a man who is down on his luck, has gambled away not only his money, but everything he has, decides to try stealing, so he breaks into the house of the Wealthy Man. He enters the room where the Nurse has

154

left the baby sleeping, and takes his time admiring the things lying around. He sees a kimono, and decides to steal it for his wife, but when he picks it up, he finds the baby wrapped in it. He becomes so interested in playing with the baby, that he doesn't think about how much noise he is making.

The Nurse hears him, and tells the Wealthy Man there is a Thief in the house. The Wealthy Man comes after him with sword drawn, and the Thief, frightened out of his wits, tries to explain his position. Finally he drops the baby and runs off pursued by the Wealthy Man. The Nurse picks up the baby, and relieved to find it unharmed, carries it off.

KOSHI INORI 腰祈
(The Back-Straightening Prayer)

I O
和 大

Shite	GRANDFATHER
Ado	YAMABUSHI
Koado	TARŌ KAJA

A Yamabushi goes to visit his Grandfather for the first time since he has become a Yamagushi. His Grandfather is very old and bent, so the Yamabushi proceeds to demonstrate his newly gained powers by praying the Grandfather's back straight. On the first attempt, the prayer is too strong so that the Grandfather can only see straight up. The next prayer, again too strong, brings the Grandfather to his knees, his back more cramped than before. The Grandfather begins to wonder if he will live through the "cure," insists on being returned to his original state, and when he can move again, chases the Yamabushi off, scolding him for treating poor old Grandfather so roughly.

Shite   KYŌTO MAN
Ado   KAMAKURA MAN

A Glue Maker from Kamakura, and one from Kyōto have
heard of each other's fame and set out to meet and see which
glue is the strongest. They meet unexpectedly on the road, and
decide to have their contest then and there.

First they tell each other the history of their own glue. The
Kamakura Man tells the story of run-away horse which was
forced to come back simply by the strength of a small amount
of his glue placed on the finger of one of his ancestors
pointed in the direction the horse had run away. As a result of
this demonstration, his glue was named "Horse Pulling
Glue." The Kyōto Man tells of a huge boulder which was
dragged by a huge number of men as far as the gate of the
garden in which it was to be used, but was to big to go through

156

the gate, so one of his ancestors made it fly over the wall by placing a little of the glue on his finger and a little on the stone. Thus his glue was named "Boulder Pulling Glue."

Next they discuss the ingredients used in their glues. The Kamakura Man claims that besides the usual ingredients, he uses the eyelashes of a thunderbolt, bamboo sprouts that grow in the sea, and an eighteen inch fang of a flea. The Kyōto Man claims that besides the usual ingredients, he uses a flying snapping turtle, a clam that grows on a tree, and a snow flake that has fallen on June thirteenth baked till it is black. (The ingredients sometimes vary.)

Both are impressed by the other's bragging, and next they decide to have a contest to see whose is the strongest. Since their ancestors used their fingers, they decide to try something new and put the glue on their noses, then see which can throw the other first. Both put up a good fight, but the Kamakura Man is finally thrown. The Kyōto Man goes off rejoicing at his triumph. The Kamakura Man picks himself up, and chases after the Kyōto Man shouting, "No fair! I slipped on a piece of resin. I demand another chance!"

KUBI HIKI 首引 (Neck Pulling)　　I O
　　　　　　　　　　　　　　　　　　　　　和 大

Shite	DEMON FATHER
Ado	TAMETOMO
Koado	DEMON PRINCESS
Tachishū	DEMONS

Tametomo, a famous warrier, meets a Demon on the road who gives him the choice of being eaten by himself or by his

157

daughter the Demon Princess. Tametomo chooses to be eaten by the Demon Princess.

The Demon Princess has never eaten a human being before, and is very shy. First she asks her Father to chew Tametomo up for her, but he says she must grow up and learn to take care of herself. She is still shy, but since he is so tasty looking, decides to have a bite. When she comes close, Tametomo taps her with his fan, and she runs crying back to her Father whimpering.

The Father Demon scolds Tametomo. The Demon Princess tries again. Tametomo taps her again, and she runs crying to her Father who is now very angry.

Tametomo asks for a chance to compete for his life in feats of strength to which the Demons finally agree. They do elbow wrestling, then ankle wrestling, but the Princess is so delicate she loses both.

Tametomo then proposes neck pulling, but the Princess is so scared of him she doesn't want to eat him anymore, to which her Father scolds her for being a disgrace to demonkind.

The Princess agrees, and when she is about to lose again, the Father calls several little Demons to help her. Tametomo wins, leaving Demons rolling all over the place. The Demon Princess goes whimpering off with her Father who tries to console her and dry her tears.

KUCHI MANE 口真似 (The Mimic)　Ｉ　Ｏ
和　大

Shite	TARŌ KAJA
Ado	MASTER
Koado	MAN (DRUNKARD)

158

The Master has received some very good *saké* as a gift, and
wants to drink it, but doesn't want to drink alone, so he calls
Tarō Kaja, and orders him to invite someone to drink with
him. Tarō Kaja, who is extremely fond of *saké*, offers to drink
with the Master, but the Master refuses him.

Tarō Kaja, rather put out, invites a well-known Drunkard,
and when the Master sees who he has brought, wants to get
rid of the Drunkard, however, not wanting to make an enemy
of the Man, instructs Tarō Kaja to do just as he does, and they
will get rid of the Man smoothly.

Tarō Kaja, still sulking, pretends to misunderstand, and
mimics every word and action of the Master. Every time the
Master scolds or strikes him, he does the same to the Man.
Finally the Master gets fed up with the whole affair, throws
Tarō Kaja down, says good-bye to the Man, and goes off
in a huff. Tarō Kaja, in turn, throws the Man down, says good-
bye, and goes off. The Man picks himself up, and goes off
wondering what it was all about.

KUCHIMANE MUKO 口真似聟
(The Mimic Groom)

和

I

Shite	GROOM
Ado	FATHER-IN-LAW
Koado	TARŌ KAJA
Koado	FRIEND (OF GROOM)

A new Groom on his way to pay his ceremonial first visit to
his Father-in-law stops by a Friend's house to ask for instructions in the proper way to carry out the ceremony. The Friend,
taking advantage of the Groom's ignorance, tells him that all

159

he needs to do is mimic everything the Father-in-law says and does to carry out the ceremony properly.

Everything goes well till the Father-in-law orders Tarō Kaja to serve *saké*. The Groom repeats the order word for word. Tarō Kaja giggles at this and is scolded by the Father-in-law, and the Groom again repeats word for word. Tarō Kaja continues to giggle, so the Father-in-law beats him, throws him down, and sends him off to the kitchen. He has just picked himself up, when the Groom catches him and gives him another beating and scolding, action for action, word for word the same as the Father-in-law.

Tarō Kaja picks himself up, and goes off in a daze, wondering what has hit him.

KUI KA HITO KA 杭か人か
(Post or Person?)

I
和

Shite	TARŌ KAJA
Ado	MASTER

The Master has heard a rumor that his servant Tarō Kaja often leaves the house when the Master goes out and leaves him to watch the place. He decides that since he can't punish Tarō Kaja just on the strength of a rumor, he will try to find out the truth for himself. He tells Tarō Kaja that he must go out this evening, goes out, but stays in the garden to see whether or not Tarō Kaja goes out.

Tarō Kaja senses that his Master's attitude was somehow different than usual, and decides he had better stay in this evening, though he has never done so before. He tries to entertain himself, but nothing seems to work, so he decides to go out and walk around the house. He has been talking to himself all this time, and the Master has been listening, getting progressively angrier. The night is very dark, and Tarō Kaja is frightened by everything he sees. He comes to the clothes line, realizes that it is the laundry flapping in the breeze, but can't quite make out whether the form near the flapping laundry is a person or a post. He asks, and the Master answers, "A post! A post!" Tarō Kaja is relieved, and starts to go on his way when the Master calls to him, scolds him for his neglect of duty and his stupidity, and chases him off.

KUJI ZAININ 鬮罪人
(Sinner by Lottery)

一〇
和 大

Shite TARŌ KAJA
Ado MASTER
Tachishū SEVERAL FRIENDS OF THE MASTER

The time for the Gion Festival is fast approaching. The Master has been appointed head of the committee for the neighborhood float for this year, so he sends Tarō Kaja to call the rest of the committee to a meeting. Everyone gathers and as the meeting begins, Tarō Kaja greets everyone, and reminds them how inadept the Master is at this sort of thing, at which he is sent out of the room.

Undaunted, Tarō Kaja listens from the next room, and objects strongly to his Master's idea of having a mountain near which is a huge wild boar which is being put down by Shirō Nitta, saying there is nothing interesting in this scene; to the next idea of having a *sumō* match on top of the mountain, saying first of all, no one fights *sumō* matches on top of mountains,

161

and secondly, there is no one in the group who would cut much of a figure in the nude fighting a *sumō* match; to another idea of building a waterfall with carp swimming upstream, reminding them that this neighborhood has used that idea so often that they have become known as the Carp Float Neighborhood. Each time Tarō Kaja comes in and objects, the Master sends him out again, and tells the others to pay him no heed. However, the others agree with his objections, and finally decide to ask Tarō Kaja for his idea.

The Master objects, but the others insist, so Tarō Kaja explains his idea while avoiding his Master's furious signals to get out.

He proposes they build two mountains, one covered with grass and foliage, and the other steep and rocky. A sinner is to appear from the green mountain, and is to be chased up and down the rocky mountain by a forbidding demon, in a lively song and dance.

The Master, of course, objects to this idea, saying it is sacrilegious, but the others think it is delightful, and decide to use it. The Master agrees reluctantly, saying there will be plenty of volunteers to play the demon, but who would want to play the sinner. Tarō Kaja says, of course it will be decided by lottery just as is done every year.

The Committee instructs Tarō Kaja to prepare the lottery. He prepares it, and each draws his part. There is one part left over, and the Committee says for Tarō Kaja himself to take it. The Master objects saying Tarō Kaja isn't qualified. The others remind him that each year, the head of the Committee uses one of his own servants. The Master says he'll hire a new servant. The Committee says there is no need to do that, and especially since it was Tarō Kaja's idea, he should be allowed to participate.

They all open the paper they have drawn, and discover what parts they have. Tarō Kaja is very happy, the others are satisfied, the Master looks at his and hurriedly folds it up again. Everyone except Tarō Kaja and the Master have announced their parts. When the Master is asked what his part is, he says he still doesn't like the whole idea, and finally that he thinks parts should be re-drawn. Tarō Kaja responds that parts for the festival are always drawn only once. One of the Committee Members grabs the Master's paper, and discovers his part is the sinner. Then Tarō Kaja gleefully announces his part is the demon.

Everyone except the Master agrees that they should have a rehearsal. The rehearsal hardly gets started when the Master chases Tarō Kaja off. The others ask what is wrong, and the Master complains that Tarō Kaja beat him. Tarō Kaja complains that the Master's ferocious looks have so unnerved him, that he can't account for his own actions, and demands that the rehearsal be done in costume with a mask so he doesn't have to see the Master's face. The Master objects, but is forced into costume.

The rehearsal proceeds. Tarō Kaja is at first afraid, but when he gets into the swing of things, begins to enjoy his part so much that the Master chases him off beating and threatening him.

In the Ōkura script, the carp suggestion is the Master's idea which Tarō Kaja says is done by another part of town every year. The next is to have the Gojō Bridge with Ushiwaka and Benkei dolls on it which Tarō Kaja also says is done by another part of town every year. The third suggestion is to build a heron bridge, and have a song and dance about it which Tarō Kaja says someone tried and failed at miserably the previous year. The rest is the same as the Izumi script.

KUMO NUSUBITO (The Spider Thief)

蜘盗人

Shite	POET
Ado	MASTER
Koado	TARŌ KAJA
Tachishū	FRIENDS OF MASTER

It is the evening for the regular meeting of a *renga* (a kind of linked poem) composing club, and all the members gather at the Master's house.

A *renga* Poet who is too poor and of too low a class, but loves *renga* more than anything else in the world, has heard of the meeting, and breaks into the house through the back fence in order to listen in on the meeting.

Tarō Kaja hears him break in, and thinking it is a thief, calls everyone in the house to help search for him. The Poet tries to hide in a thicket in the garden, and gets caught in a spider's nest.

He is found and he explains his situation. The Master says he will only believe his story if he can compose an acceptable line to a poem. He performs very skillfully, and the Master not only orders Tarō Kaja to help him get loose, but invites him to join their club. *Saké* is served, and all have a merry time.

When the Poet gets ready to leave, the Master gives him a *kimono*, and invites him to come not only to club meetings, but any time at all, and not through the back fence, but the front door.

The Poet expresses his gratitude in a song and dance about his good luck and the Master's kind hospitality.

In the Ōkura script, the Master presents the Poet with a sword instead of a *kimono*. The rest is the same as the Izumi script.

164

KURAMA MAIRI 鞍馬参
(The Blessing Transfer)

Shite TARŌ KAJA
Ado MASTER

It is early in the new year, and the Master calls Tarō Kaja to accompany him on his yearly pilgrimage to the Kurama Shrine. When they arrive, the Master says he will not go to the inn as usual, but will spend the night at the shrine, and orders Tarō Kaja to sit up, and wake him when the sky becomes white.

Tarō Kaja, of course, wants to get some sleep too. He wakes the Master on various pretexts until the Master finally tells him to sleep too.

Tarō Kaja dreams that an eighty year old priest dressed in red robes with a red hat and crystal rosary comes and blesses him. The Master wants to receive this blessing since he didn't have a dream, so he says that he had a dream in which he was told that he was to receive the blessing from Tarō Kaja.

Tarō Kaja says that method of transferring the blessing is by performing a song and dance, which he teaches to his Master. They go off singing and dancing together in celebration of their New Year blessing.

KURAMA MUKO 鞍馬聟
(The Groom from Kurama)

Shite GROOM FROM KURAMA
Ado FATHER-IN-LAW
Koado TARŌ KAJA
Koado WIFE OF SHITE

The Father-in-law has two married daughters. The younger lives in the capital, and visits her father often. The Older daughter lives in Kurama, and not only has not been home since she was married four or five years before, but her husband has not yet made his ceremonial first visit to her Father's house.

The Kurama Groom has to see some of his customers in the capital, and decides to take this opportunity to make the ceremonial visit. The whole family including the younger daughter's Groom is waiting in expectation, but when the Kurama Groom is introduced to the Groom from the capital, he turns and runs out of the house.

When his Wife comes out to inquire what happened, he explains that many years before, he had cheated the Groom from the capital in a business deal, and they had fought over it. He wants to go home immediately, but his Wife convinces him to bandage his head so the other Groom won't recognize him, explain that he was stung by a bee, and carry out the ceremony.

Everything goes well, and after the ceremony, they all begin drinking. The Father-in-law asks the Groom from the capital to dance, after which he asks the Kurama Groom to perform something. The Kurama Groom says that the only thing he can perform well is *sumō*, and adds that he has never been beaten. The Groom from the capital agrees to wrestle with him, and throws him with very little effort.

The Kurama Groom picks himself up in a daze, and grabs for his wife saying, "At least, I know I can beat you." Instead of his Wife, it is Tarō Kaja he has grabbed. Tarō Kaja gets loose, and runs off like a scared rabbit, with the Kurama Groom close at his heels shouting, "Come back and fight, you coward!"

KURIKUMA SHINMEI   栗隈神明
(*See* Imajinmei)

KURI YAKI 栗焼 (Roasting Chestnuts)   I O
和 大

Shite   TARŌ KAJA
Ado   MASTER

The Master calls Tarō Kaja, and orders him to roast forty chestnuts that he has received from his uncle. Since there are many guests expected, the chestnuts should be roasted carefully.

Tarō Kaja finds a charcoal fire in the kitchen, and thoroughly enjoys roasting them. When he finishes, they look so delicious that he can't resist tasting just one, then another, and another till they are all gone.

When his Master asks for the chestnuts, Tarō Kaja tells him that the god and goddess of pots and pans, in the form of an old man and woman, appeared with an entourage of thirty people, and demanded the chestnuts. He gave two each to the god and goddess, and one apiece to each of the others, which left only one which was rotten. The Master points out that his arithmetic is faulty, and that there should be three left, to which Tarō Kaja replies that they were lost in the fire. The Master chases him off scolding.

KUSABIRA 茸 (Mushrooms)

Shite	YAMABUSHI
Ado	MAN
Tachishū	ELEVEN MUSHROOMS

A Man calls a Yamabushi to help him get rid of some Mushrooms that have been growing in his house. These are not ordinary mushrooms, but huge ones that look like a man wearing a straw hat or carrying an umbrella.

The Yamabushi comes to the Man's house, and begins praying, but instead of going away, the Mushrooms begin to increase until finally the whole house is filled with them.

An especially large Mushroom appears, and leads the others in chasing the Man and the Yamabushi out of the house.

MAGO MUKO 孫聟
(The Grandson Groom)

Shite	OLD GRANDFATHER
Ado	FATHER-IN-LAW
Koado	TARŌ KAJA
3rd Ado	GROOM

It is the day that the new Groom is expected to make his ceremonial first visit to his Father-in-law. The Father-in-law and Tarō Kaja are busy preparing for the visit. The Old Grandfather has become childish in his old age, and is a terrible nuisance, so they are trying to plan some way to get him out of the house until the ceremony is finished. The Grandfather hears their conversation, and refuses to leave the house. They send him to his room and promise to call him when the Groom arrives.

The Groom arrives and asks to see the Grandfather before the ceremony begins. The Grandfather offers the Groom cup after cup of *saké* and invites him to his room to drink together and talk. The Father-in-law and Tarō Kaja make repeated attempts to get rid of the Grandfather with no success. In fact, he hardly gives them a chance to perform the ceremony.

The ceremony is finally completed, and they all begin to sing and dance in celebration. The Grandfather joins in the singing and dancing, and they all leave him alone when he is not looking. When he realizes he has been left alone, he goes off grumbling about their inconsiderate attitude.

MAKURA MONOGURUI 枕物狂 （Grandfather in Love）

和 大 I O

Shite	GRANDFATHER
Ado	GRANDSON I (TARŌ)
Koado	GRANDSON II (JIRŌ)

Tarō and Jirō go to visit their Grandfather, who is over one hundred years old, because they have heard that he has fallen in love and lost his mind. They want to help him if there is any way they can.

When they arrive at their Grandfather's house, he is lost in a reverie, singing about his love. When they get his attention, he scolds them for neglecting him and they apologize. He asks them why they have come, and they say they have heard he has fallen in love and lost his mind. He laughs at them and

169

denies it, but says he will tell them a love story. During the telling of the story, it is obvious that he himself is greatly moved, and the Grandsons bring this to his attention when he has finished. They assure him that they only wish to do what they can to help him, so he consents to tell them the whole story if they will promise not to tell anyone.

The Grandfather admits he has fallen in love with the youngest daughter of Gyubū Saburō named Oto. He sings about her beauty and his love for her. During his song, Tarō and Jirō go out and bring Oto to visit him which makes him very happy.

MARI ZATŌ 鞠座頭 　　　　　イ　オ

(Blind Man's Football) 　　　　　和　大

Shite	BLIND MASTER
Ado	KIKUICHI (SHITE'S SERVANT, ALSO BLIND)
Tchishū	NINE BLIND MEN
Koado	PASSER-BY

Nine Blind Men meet at the Blind Master's house for a meeting to practice the singing done by blind men as a profession at that time. One of them performs a chanted narrative (*katari*) for Kikuichi. They drink *saké* and finish the business of their meeting. They decide to play some game or other for recreation. Several suggestions such as *go*, *shōgi*, and *sugoroku* (all are Japanese games played with different kinds of pieces on a checked board), but all are rejected because of the difficulty involved in playing without eyesight.

They finally decide to play a kind of football, and in order to locate the ball when it falls, they tie a small bell to it. They are enjoying themselves when a Passer-by comes along, and decides to tease them. He picks up the ball, and runs here and there ringing the bell. They all chase after the sound of the bell, kick at space, and fall all over themselves and each other. The Passer-by enjoys this spectacle so much that he inadvertently laughs out loud. They discover the truth and chase after him with their canes, running into and mistaking each other for the Culprit.

In the Ōkura script, the Blind Men meet for the purpose of playing football. They immediately put the bell on the ball and begin to play. The Passer-by does not laugh out loud, and is not discovered. He simply leaves with the ball when he gets tired of teasing the Blind Men. They realize the ball is gone and chase off in search of it, bumping into each other, etc., the same as in the Izumi script.

MATSU BAYASHI　松囃子
(The Song and Dance of the Pine)

Shite　　BANZAI TARŌ

I
和

171

| Ado | RICH MAN I (YOUNGER BROTHER) |
| Koado | RICH MAN II (OLDER BROTHER) |

Two rich brothers are waiting for Banzai Tarō who comes every New Year's Day to bless their houses with song and dance. He finally comes, and they accuse him of being late. Tarō says he is not late at all, they have just forgotten when he usually comes. He dances, and they complain that his dance and song are much shorter than usual. He claims that it is the same as always. Tarō finally gets across to them, by way of polite hints, that the previous year they forgot to give him the usual gift of money in return for his song and dance. They apologize for being forgetful, and give him an especially large gift. All ends happily with an especially large song and dance blessing from Tarō.

MATSU YANI 松脂   I O
(The Spirit of Pine Resin)   和 大

Shite	SPIRIT OF PINE RESIN
Ado	MASTER
Koado	TARŌ KAJA
Tachishū	GUESTS

The Master sends Tarō Kaja to call the Guests for the New Year Celebration. They gather, and decide to sing and dance in praise of Pine Resin. The Spirit of Pine Resin appears, thinking he has been called by them. They ask him to tell the virtues of the pine which he does in a chanted narrative (*katari*). They decide to catch him, and mix the resin with oil as a dressing for bows. He sings and dances telling them the best method for using Pine Resin.

MATSU YUZURIHA 松樗 I O 和大
(One Hat for Two)

Shite	FARMER FROM TSU
Ado	FARMER FROM TANBA
Koado	TAX COLLECTOR

Two Farmers on their way to the capital to pay their annual taxes meet on the road, and decide to travel together. After they pay their taxes, they are given one *eboshi* (a lacquered ceremonial hat) between the two of them as a reward.

The Tax Collector orders them to put on the hat and appear before him. One of them does so, then the Tax Collector asks for the other to appear. This exchange is done several times. The Tax Collector finally orders them to appear together. Then he scolds them because only one has a hat on. They put the one hat on together which results in their being tied together. He orders them to sing and dance on their way home. Thus they go off singing and dancing happily tied together.

In the Ōkura script, the hat is not presented to the Farmers. They are ordered to compose poems, then sing them and dance on the way home. The rest is the same as the Izumi script.

MEJIKA 目近 I O 和大
(Fans of Mistaken Identity)

Shite	WEALTHY MAN
Ado	TARŌ KAJA

173

Koado   JIRŌ KAJA
Koado   FAN SELLER

A Wealthy Man orders his two servants, Tarō Kaja and Jirō Kaja, to go to the capital to buy a *mejika* and a *komehone*. They get to the capital, and realize that neither one of them know what these things are, so they begin shouting that they want to buy a *mejika* and a *komehone*, hoping someone who knows what they are will hear them, and come to their aid. (*Mejika* means "close to the eyes," and *komehone* means "full of sticks.")

A dishonest Fan Seller decides to cheat them. He sells them two old fans telling them that *komehone* means that there is rice in the sticks, thus making the fan special (*kome* means "rice"), and the other fan he sticks under their noses telling them that the only difference between the two is that the *mejika* is presented to a person by sticking it under his nose. He also teaches them a song as a special gift to please their Master when he is angry. They take their new possessions

174

home, and explain the meaning to the Master. He gets angry, and tells them that a *komehone* is simply a fan with more sticks than usual, and a *mejika* is a fan with the rivet placed differently. Then he chases them out. They begin singing and dancing. The Master hears them, comes out to watch, forgives them, and rewards them for their clever song.

MI KAZUKI 箕被   I O
(The Winnow Basket Hat)   和 大

     Shite   POET
     Ado   WIFE

A Poet tells his Wife to prepare for guests because he has invited his friends to have a *renga* (a kind of linked poem) making meeting. She refuses saying there is nothing in the house to feed them, and besides she insists that he give up composing poetry all the time, and go to work. This develops into an argument which ends in her asking for a divorce. He says, "First listen to a story I have to tell you." And he tells a story about a Chinese Poet who was poor and had a wife who scolded at him to go to work, but he stuck to his studies and writing, and finally became a famous poet and a minister in the service of the Emperor.

She still insists on leaving, and asks for something to take with her. He gives her the winnow basket that she always uses, because there is nothing left in the house. She puts the basket on her head and starts away. He recites the first line of a poem as she leaves. She comes back to add the second line, because there is a proverb to the effect that if you don't answer when someone gives you the first line of a poem, you will be born

175

as a mouth-less insect in your next incarnation. He begs her to stay, promising he will give up poetry and go to work. She finally consents, and they drink and sing and dance in celebration of their reunion.

MIZU KAKE MUKO　水掛聟
(The Water Throwing Son-in-law)

Shite	SON-IN-LAW
Ado	FATHER-IN-LAW
Koado	WOMAN (WIFE OF SHITE)

A Son-in-law comes to tend his rice paddy, and finds that all the water has been drained off to the neighboring paddy. He redirects the water, and leaves to take care of his other paddies. His Father-in-law (who owns the neighboring paddy) comes along and again redirects the water to his own paddy. The Son-in-law returns, catches him in the act, and they have

176

an argument which develops into a water fight, and finally an all-out mud throwing brawl. The Wife of the Son-in-law appears on the scene, and is ordered by both to help out in the fight. She sides with her husband. The Father-in-law is beaten and thrown down in the mud. As he picks himself up, he cries out after them that in return for this, they will no longer be invited to take part in the annual festival.

In the Ōkura script, the order of appearance of the Groom and the Father-in-law is opposite, thus it is the Father-in-law who catches the Groom in the act. At the end of the play, the Father-in-law says that if they don't treat their elders better than this, they will have a black future. The rest is the same as the Izumi script.

MIZU KUMI 水汲 (Drawing Water)　　　I　O
(Ōkura title: Ocha no Mizu お茶の水　　　和　大

| Shite | ACOLYTE |
| Ado | TEMPLE MAID |

The Temple Maid goes to the spring in the field to do the laundry, and the Acolyte goes to draw water for tea. The Acolyte asks the Temple Maid to draw the water for him, and convinces her to do it by saying that it will be sweeter if she draws it. She consents and they sing together as she draws the water. He wants to make love after the water is drawn, but she says that the water must be taken back to the temple first. He tries to embrace her, and she accidentally spills the water on him. They go on their way, wet but happy.

In the Ōkura script, there are three characters, the third being the Head Priest.

The Head Priest calls the Acolyte and orders him to go draw water, since it is too dark for the Temple Maid to go. The Acolyte refuses saying it doesn't matter how dark it may be, water drawing is the work of the Temple Maid. The Head Priest sends the Temple Maid for the water. The Acolyte sneaks out after her. They tease each other and make love, singing and enjoying themselves. The Head Priest gets worried when the Temple Maid doesn't come back, goes out to see what has happened to her, and finds them together. The Head Priest begins to beat the Acolyte. The Temple Maid helps the Acolyte, and they throw the Head Priest down and go off happily together. He picks himself up and calls out after them, "You will surely have bad luck for this!"

This is the only Kyōgen which deals with love between an unmarried couple.

MOCHIZAKE 餅酒 (Late Taxes) I 和

Shite	FARMER FROM ECHIZEN
Ado	FARMER FROM KAGA
Koado	TAX COLLECTOR

Two Farmers come to the capital to pay their annual taxes. One is a *Saké* Maker from Echizen, and the other is a *Mochi* (rice cake) Maker from Kaga. They meet on the road, decide to travel together, and upon arrival find that their destination is the same. They were not able to come sooner because of a bad snow storm, so they are bringing the late tax from the previous year along with the present year's tax. In punishment for coming late, they are required to make a poem using the

178

name of their own product, after which they laugh so loud and long, that they are required to compose and sing a longer poem. Then they are ordered to sing and dance these poems on the way home. They go off singing and dancing together.

MORAI MUKO 貰聟
(The Repentant Husband)

Shite	YOUNG MAN (GROOM)
Ado	WOMAN (WIFE OF SHITE)
Koado	FATHER-IN-LAW

A Young Man comes home drunk, fights with his Wife, and sends her home to her Father giving her a dagger as a sign that this time, his desire for a divorce is final. It appears that this is not the first time this sort of thing has happened. When she reaches her Father's house, she tearfully declares that she will never return to her Husband, and her Father swears that he will

never allow her to return.

The next morning when the Young Man has sobered up, and the baby cries for its mother, he goes to get his Wife back, but the Father insists that she is not in his house. The Husband swears that he will never drink another drop of liquor, and will never try to divorce her again, and that the baby is helpless without its Mother. The Father-in-law still claims he doesn't know where she is. The Wife, moved by her Husband's tears, appears and says she will go back with him. The Father-in-law gets angry, and tries to force her to stay. The Husband and Wife finally throw the old Father-in-law down and go happily on their way home. The Father-in-law picks himself up and shouts after them that beginning next year, they will not be allowed to participate in the village festival.

MUNE TSUKI 胸突   I O
(Punched in the Chest)   和 大

| Shite | MAN I |
| Ado | MAN II |

Man II goes to Man I's house determined to collect a long overdue debt. Man I realizes who it is at the door, and pretends to be out. Man II catches him anyway, grabs him by his lapels, and threatens him. Man I continues to make excuses, and trys to put Man II off. Man II finally gets angry, punches Man I in the chest and knocks him down.

Man I pretends to be mortally wounded. Man II gets worried because of the noise Man I is making, and says he will deduct the interest on the loan, if Man I will only settle down. Man I real-

izes he has a good thing going, and begins to howl louder till Man II not only says he will forget the loan entirely, but also returns the IOU which Man I immediately tears to shreds.

As Man II helps Man I up, Man I breaks into gales of laughter. Man II says, "But I thought you were about to die." Man I answers, "Yeh, I was about to die worrying whether or not I'd be able to get this IOU away from you." He runs off laughing merrily, followed closely by Man II shouting, "Just wait till I catch you, you dirty thief!"

NABE YATSUBACHI　鍋八撥 I O
(Pots and Drums)　　　和 大

Shite　SELLER OF EARTHENWARE POTS
Ado　OFFICIAL IN CHARGE OF THE MARKET
Koado　SELLER OF DRUMS

181

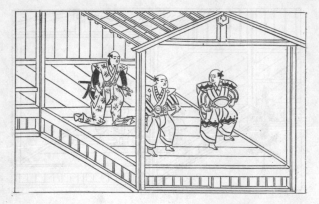

The Official appears and puts up a sign saying that the merchant who arrives first on the day of the local fair will be awarded the most desirable position for setting up his booth. A Drum Seller appears, and finding it still dark, confident of having been the first to arrive, decides to take a "cat nap" while waiting for the sun and the other merchants.

An Earthenware Pot Seller appears, and seeing the Drum Seller sleeping decides to try to cheat him out of the prize. He pretends to sleep.

When the official arrives, both claim to have arrived first. The Official asks for proof from both that their respective products are superior since he can't decide which is telling the truth. The Drum Seller recites a poem praising drums and the Pot Seller sings a song praising pots. Both poem and song are very good, so the decision is still not reached. The Official then decides that they must compete for the prize.

The Drum Seller is first, and presents feats which are easy for him but difficult for the Pot Seller. Finally the Drum Seller turns cartwheels off the stage. When the Pot Seller tries to do the same, he falls on his pot which breaks. He picks up the pieces and says, "What good luck! Now instead of one, I have many!" (In case the pot doesn't break he says, "This is certainly a well-baked pot. I will take it home and keep it as a treasure.")

NAGAMITSU 長光 ILO 和大
(The Sword Nagamitsu)

Shite	SHYSTER
Ado	COUNTRY MAN
Koado	ARBITER

A Country Man comes to the capital for the first time. He has brought a very valuable sword called Nagamitsu, to deliver to someone. While he is looking around the market, a Shyster slips up behind him, and slips the end of the sword into his own belt. When the Country Man notices what has hap-

pened, they begin to quarrel, both, of course, claiming the sword. An Arbiter appears and tries to settle the fight. The Shyster eavesdrops while the Country Man is telling his side of the story, and tells exactly the same story when it comes his turn.

Finally the Arbiter asks the measurements of the sword which the Country Man whispers in his ear. The Shyster can't answer correctly since he wasn't able to hear. He accuses the Arbiter of favoring the Country Man unfairly, and starts off, saying, "But then, what's the loss of one sword anyway!" They grab him, and when they begin to beat him, find many other things he has stolen under his cloak. They beat him and chase him off.

In the Ōkura script, the Country Man has been in the capital for a long time, and goes to the market to buy souvenirs for his family, because he is going home soon. The sword Nagamitsu is his own. The Shyster's attitude at the end is one of apology in the Izumi script, but of indignation in the Ōkura.

NAGINATA ASHIRAI 長刀応答 I
(The Halberd Welcome) 和

Shite	TARŌ KAJA
Ado	MASTER
Koado	FLOWER VIEWER
Koado	SEVERAL FLOWER VIEWERS

The Master goes out, and leaves Tarō Kaja to watch the house, and keep all intruders out by chasing them away with a halberd.

It is spring, and the Master's garden is famous for its beautiful spring flowers. Several Flower Viewers come to view the flowers, and Tarō Kaja lets them in, but immediately chases them out with his halberd. The Flower Viewers all get together, decide that Tarō Kaja must have gone crazy, and go in a group to take his halberd away from him.

They get Tarō Kaja's halberd from him, throw him down, and leave. He yells after them, "How can I entertain guests without my halberd? Give it back to me!"

NAKI AMA 泣尼 (The Crying Nun)　　　I O
　　　　　　　　　　　　　　　　　　　　和大

Shite	PRIEST
Ado	MAN
Koado	NUN

A Man comes in from the country in search of a Priest to bless the memorial he has built for his dead father. He stops at

185

the first temple he comes to and presents his case. The Priest makes excuses and refuses until he finds that the Man plans to give a very large donation in return for the services.

The Priest is very poor at preaching and performing ceremonies, so he invites a Nun who is well known for bursting into tears upon the slightest provocation. He finally convinces her to come along by offering her a ten percent commission.

The Priest and the Nun go to the country with the Man. When the Priest begins his sermon, the Nun, instead of crying, immediately goes to sleep. The Priest tries in vain to wake her by coughing loudly and using the words tear (*namida*) and cry (*naku*) over and over in his sermon. The Nun finally wakes up with a start when the Priest strikes the gong indicating the end of his sermon.

On the way home, the Nun praises the Priest for his sermon and cries. Then she asks for her commission. The Priest says, "No tears, no commission." The Nun grabs ahold of him, and tries to throw him down. The Priest knocks the Nun down and leaves. The Nun chases after the Priest complaining in a loud voice, very much awake at last.

In the Ōkura script, the Man goes to a Priest he has recently met to ask him to perform the ceremony. The Priest readily agrees. Since he has never performed this kind of ceremony before, he asks the crying Nun to go with him. He convinces her to go by offering her half his pay for the ceremony. The rest is the same as the Izumi script.

NAMAGUSAMONO 腥物 (A Raw Fish)   I
和

Shite   TARŌ KAJA

Ado   MASTER
Koado   PASSER-BY

A Master sends Tarō Kaja to return his uncle's sword which he had borrowed for the festival. He has wrapped the sword in straw, and tied it with a vine to disguise it. He tells Tarō Kaja that if anyone on the road should ask him what he is carrying, he should say that it is just a raw fish, and definitely not to tell them it is a ceremonial gold sword for fear of its being stolen.

Tarō Kaja goes on his way and meets a Passer-by, and sure enough the Passer-by asks him what he is carrying. He says it is not a gold sword, but only a raw fish. The Passer-by demands it or his life. Tarō Kaja throws his package down and takes to his heels. The Passer-by calls after him that he will be back that way the next day, so Tarō Kaja had better not be in the area if he values his life.

Tarō Kaja reaches home and tells his Master what has happened, claiming he did not say anything about it being a sword. The Master scolds him and says they must retrieve the sword. They wait in ambush, catch the Passer-by on his return trip, and get the sword back. The Master holds the culprit by the arms, and orders Tarō Kaja to bring a rope to tie him up. The Passer-by struggles and kicks. The Master complains at the time Tarō Kaja is taking. Tarō Kaja finally gets the rope twisted and ready, and tries to tie the Passer-by up. The Passer-by kicks Tarō Kaja, so the Master suggests tying him from behind. Tarō Kaja tells the Master he has got the rope on securely, so he can let go. The Master lets go, and the Passer-by runs off, but the Master cannot move because Tarō Kaja, in the confusion, has tied the Master instead of the Passer-by.

187

NARIAGARI 成上り
(A Strange Evolution)

Shite	TARŌ KAJA
Ado	MASTER
Koado	SHYSTER

A Master takes Tarō Kaja on his annual New Year's pilgrimage to a temple where they spend the night. During the night, a Shyster steals the ceremonial sword, and leaves a bamboo stick in its place.

When the Master and Tarō Kaja wake up, Tarō Kaja sees what has happened, and quickly hides the stick behind his back. The Master says it is time to return home, but Tarō Kaja suggests that they sit and talk for a while since it is still dark.

Tarō Kaja suggests they talk about evolutions and advancements. The Master thinks he is talking about natural advancements such as a man being promoted, etc., but Tarō Kaja wants to talk about more unusual evolutions such as mountain potatoes evolving into eels, frogs evolving into beetles, and brides evolving into mothers-in-law. Finally he tells the story of a man who went hunting and forgot to take his sword. He saw a serpent in the eye of one of the men with him which on closer investigation turned out to be the sword he had forgotten. Then Tarō Kaja says that his Master's sword seems to have evolved in the opposite direction while they were sleeping, and shows him the bamboo stick.

The Master says that someone must have stolen it, and if so, is probably still in the area stealing things from other people sleeping there. They hide and wait. Sure enough the Shyster appears once more. They catch him and retrieve the sword.

188

The Master holds him while Tarō Kaja twists the rope to tie him with.

The Shyster struggles and kicks. The Master complains at the time Tarō Kaja is taking. Tarō Kaja finally gets the rope ready, and tries to tie the Shyster up from the front. The Shyster kicks Tarō Kaja, so the Master suggests tying him from the back. Tarō Kaja agrees, gets the rope tied, and tells the Master he can let go. The Master lets go, and the Shyster takes off at a dead run, but the Master cannot move because Tarō Kaja, in the confusion, has tied up his Master instead of the Shyster.

In the Ōkura script, the discussion about various evolutions is done on the way home, and the play ends when Tarō Kaja shows the Master the bamboo stick, and the Master scolds him soundly for his negligence.

NARIHIRA MOCHI　業平餅　　　I O
(The Poet and the Rice Cakes)　　和 大

Shite	NARIHIRA
Ado	RICE CAKE SELLER
Koado	PAGE
Koado	DAUGHTER (OF RICE CAKE SELLER)
Koado	RETAINER
Koado	RETAINER
Koado	RETAINER
Koado	UMBRELLA BEARER

Ariwara Narihira, a famous poet nobleman of the Heian Period, starts out with his entourage on a pilgrimage to Tamatsushima. They enjoy the scenery and compose poems as they

189

go happily along. They reach a Rice Cake Shop near a beach, and Narihira decides to stop there for refreshment.

The Rice Cake Seller appears, and offers them his rice cakes. Narihira says, "You mean you will let anyone have your rice cakes?" The Rice Cake Seller replies, "Of course, if they put out the necessary cash." (*Oashi* means both "cash" and "foot.") Narihira sticks out one foot. The Rice Cake Seller laughs and says, "Not one foot, money!" (*Ryōsoku* means both "money" and "both feet.") Narihira sticks out both feet. The Rice Seller explains that he must have legal tender which Narihira finally understands, and responds, "I never touch anything so filthy." (Noblemen of the period considered it very unsophisticated to even talk about money, let alone touch or carry it.)

Narihira tells in a chanted narrative (*katari*) how Ono Komachi, a famous and beautiful poetess, received rice cakes in payment for a poem which caused it to rain on a certain occasion. On the strength of this story, he offers a poem in payment of the rice cakes.

The Rice Cake Seller finally realizes who his customer is, and since Narihira is famous not only as a poet, but even more so as a lady's man, always on the lookout for attractive girls, asks him to take his daughter into service. Narihira urges the the Rice Cake Seller to go fetch her immediately.

While the Rice Cake Seller is gone, Narihira, whose hunger at this point is much stronger than his interest in the girl, begins stuffing his mouth with the Rice Cakes. By the time the Rice Cake Seller returns with his daughter, Narihira is choking. The Rice Cake Seller tells him he should eat more slowly because he can have all the rice cakes he desires. He presents his daughter, and leaves her with Narihira so the two can get better acquainted.

When Narihira sees the girl's face, which is extremely ugly,

190

he tries to pawn her off on his Umbrella Bearer, but the Umbrella Bearer doesn't want her either. They try to get away, but she follows after them demanding justice.

NARUKO 鳴子 (Bird Clappers)

Shite	TARŌ KAJA
Ado	MASTER
Koado	JIRŌ KAJA

The Master orders Tarō Kaja and Jirō Kaja to take the bird clappers and go to the rice paddies where the grain is ripening to scare away birds and beasts. They object that this is work for women and children, but the Master says that since the rice paddies are in the mountains, women and children would be too frightened of the wild boars and monkeys, and would probably run away. Then they suggest he send only one of them to which he answers he is sure one of them alone would get very bored.

They reach the rice paddies, set up their bird clappers, and are enjoying themselves chatting and scaring away birds when the Master come with a barrel of saké which he suggests they use to help the time pass more quickly.

The Master returns home, and Tarō Kaja and Jirō Kaja begin drinking and singing.They try their best to keep one eye on their work, and finally decide that the best way is to tie the bird clapper cords around their waists so they can manipulate them from where they are sitting.

After they have drunk all the saké, they sing and dance together praising their kind Master, giving thanks for the good harvest and the good weather, and generally expressing their happiness. After this, they are so exhausted that they untie the cords and lie down for a nap, one using the *saké* barrel for a pillow, the other its lid.

When it gets dark and they still haven't returned home, the Master goes out to see what happened to them. He finds them dead asleep, and shouts that there are birds all over the field. They wake up startled, and in their confusion grab the *saké* barrel and lid, and begin shaking them in place of the clappers. The Master half-jokingly chases them off scolding.

NARUKO YARUKO 鳴子遣子 I O
(The Bird Clapper Quarrel) 和 大

Shite	TEA SHOP OWNER
Ado	MAN I
Koado	MAN II

Two Men start out to visit a temple together. On the way they see some bird clappers being used in a field along the road. Man I calls them *naruko*, but Man II insists that they are called *yaruko*. They bet their swords, and go ask the Tea Shop Owner to mediate.

They both talk to him privately, and he tells them both they are actually wrong. Man I bribes him with a new tea pot (a basket of charcoal in the Ōkura script), and Man II bribes him with a load of fire wood.

The Tea Shop Owner tells a story in chanted narrative (*katari*) which includes both names, thus the argument cannot be settled, so the Tea Shop Owner runs off with both swords saying, "When an argument cannot be settled, the mediator gets the spoils." The two Men chase after him demanding justice.

NATORIGAWA 名取川
(The Name Stealing River)

I O
和 大

| Shite | PRIEST |
| Ado | VILLAGER FROM NATORI |

A Priest has just come from Mount Hiei where he was given a name in token of becoming a full-fledged priest. He is very forgetful, so he asked for a spare name in case he forgets the first one, and then had one name written on each of his sleeves. He comes to a wide muddy river. After he crosses it, he discovers that the names have been washed off his sleeves in the water, and he has forgotten both of them. A Villager comes along, and the Priest questions him. He says that the river is called the Name Stealing River (Natorigawa), the village is called Name Stealer, and the family name of the people is Name Stealer.

The Priest accuses the Villager of stealing his names, and refuses to let him go till he returns them. The villager says, "You certainly say uncommon (*kitai*) things." At which the Priest recalls his first name, Kitai-Bō. The Priest insists on the other name also, and again the Villager inadvertently uses the word "unknown" (*fushō*), which is the Priest's other name, Fushō-Bō. The Priest goes happily on his way, constantly repeating the two names so as not to forget them again.

193

NAWA NAI 縄綯 (Rope Twisting)

Shite	TARŌ KAJA
Ado	OLD MASTER
Koado	NEW MASTER

Tarō Kaja's Master loves gambling, but is very poor at it. So poor at it that he loses not only all his money and possessions, but finally Tarō Kaja as well.

The Old Master knows that Tarō Kaja will object if he tells him the truth, so he tricks him by sending him with a letter to his New Master's place. Tarō Kaja is very put out at being tricked as well as being used as collateral, so he pretends he cannot do any of the work he is ordered to do.

The New Master gets angry, and returns Tarō Kaja. The Old Master has the New Master hide and watch, while he has Tarō Kaja twist a rope, to prove he can do good work.

While Tarō Kaja is working, he tells about the bad working conditions, and the terrible mistress and children at the New Master's house. He, of course, doesn't know the New Master is listening. Finally the New Master can take it no longer. He beats Tarō Kaja and chases him off.

NEGI YAMABUSHI 禰宜山伏
(The Negi and the Yamabushi)

Shite	YAMABUSHI
Ado	NEGI (SHINTŌ PRIEST)
Koado	TEA SHOP OWNER
Koado	DAIKOKU (STATUE)

194

A Negi stops by the tea shop of a Friend of his on his way to the capital. They are drinking tea and chatting pleasantly when a Yamabushi comes storming in and orders tea. He complains, first that it is too hot, then that it is too cool. He notices the Negi, pushes him off his stool, and sits on it himself. They begin insulting each other until the Negi gets frightened and tries to run away through the back door, to which the Tea Shop Owner objects, saying that he would then be in trouble because the Yamabushi has been insisting that the Negi carry his luggage.

The Tea Shop Owner suggests they compete by seeing who can make a Statue of Daikoku (one of the seven happy gods) face his way by praying. The Negi tries first, and the Statue immediately faces his way. The Yamabushi tries, and the Statue faces away from him, and when he tries to force it to turn his way, it hits him on the head with its hammer. The Tea Shop Owner announces that the Negi has won, but the Yamabushi objects saying that the Owner has been on the Negi's side all along, so they decide to try once more, this time they both pray at the same time. The Daikoku Statue immediately turns toward the Negi. The Yamabushi tries several times to force it to turn his way, and gets hit over the head each time. Finally the Statue gets up, and brandishing its hammer, chases the Yamabushi off. The Negi runs after them shouting, "I've won! You must carry my luggage!"

NE ONGYOKU　寝音曲
(Horizontal Singing)

I　O
和　大

| Shite | TARŌ KAJA |
| Ado | MASTER |

The Master happened to pass by Tarō Kaja's room the previous night and heard him singing in a loud clear voice. He calls Tarō Kaja and orders him to sing. Tarō Kaja says the only time he can sing is when he is drunk, so the Master brings out *saké*. Tarō Kaja drinks and drinks, but doesn't offer to sing. When the Master reminds him that he is to sing, Tarō Kaja says that after getting drunk, he must lie down with his wife's knee for a pillow in order to be able to sing. The Master offers his own knee, Tarō Kaja pretends his Master is his wife, and sings a very short song.

The Master orders him to try to sing sitting, then standing, but he pretends not to be able to make a sound. The Master is determined to hear him sing once more, so he offers his knee again.

While Tarō Kaja is singing, the Master makes him sit up, and he stops, lays him down again, and he begins again. The Master does this several times, and with increasing speed, till Tarō

Kaja gets dizzy and begins to sing when he is up and stop when he is down. Finally he stands, and does a dance while singing.

The Master chases him off scolding him for lying.

NIKUJŪHACHI 二九十八 (2918)

I O
和 大

| Shite | MAN |
| Ado | NEW WIFE |

A Man goes to the Kiyomizu Temple to pray for a Wife. He is told in a dream that he will find her on the steps at the Western Gate. He finds her, and asks where she lives. She speaks in poetic riddles, and tells him that she lives in Muromachi Kasugamachi. He asks which house and she answers, "Two nine." He figures two nines make eighteen, goes to the eighteenth house and finds her there. He takes her hand and leads her happily to his house. He asks her to take off her veil, she refuses, he insists, and finally takes it off himself. He is surprised and disappointed when he looks at her face, because she is very ugly. He runs off trying to get away, and she chases after him.

In the Ōkura script, the Man makes excuses trying to get away, but she won't let him go. He finally tells her she is so ugly he can't stand being near her, throws her down, and runs off. She gets up and chases out after him.

NIŌ (The Fake Deva King)

I O

仁王

| Shite | MAN (NIŌ) |

和 大

Ado	FRIEND (OF SHITE)
Koado	CRIPPLE
Tachishū	SEVERAL WORSHIPPERS

A Man who loves to gamble has had a run of bad luck and lost everything he owns. He decides to leave the country and try to make a living somewhere else. Before he goes, he stops by to tell his best Friend good-bye.

The Friend suggests that they dress him up as a Deva King (niō), put him in a deserted area, and he himself will go tell everyone that a statue of a Deva King with magic powers has descended from the heavens. People will then come to pray and bring gifts. The Man thinks this is a good idea, but before the Friend will help him carry it out, he makes him promise to give up gambling, and take up some honest profession.

They dress him up, set him up as a statue in the deserted area, and the Friend brings a group of Worshippers who pray and leave various gifts. After they have gone, the Friend takes the gifts home saying the news will spread, and there will undoubtedly be more worshippers soon.

Presently a Cripple comes who believes that if one rubs the various parts of a sacred statue, then rubs the same parts of one's own body, one will become well and strong. He begins rubbing the Deva King's body here and there. The Man who is the statue is very ticklish, so he isn't able to hold still. The Cripple discovers the truth, and chases the Statue off yelling, "Fake! Fake!"

In the Ōkura script, the first group of Worshippers comes back a second time bringing the Cripple. They notice that the Statue moves when the Cripple rubs it. They discover the truth, tickle him, then chase him off. The Cripple limps off last, shouting, "Treating a poor Cripple this way will give you nothing but bad luck in the future!"

NIWATORI MUKO 鶏聟
(The Rooster Groom)

I O
和 大

Shite	GROOM
Ado	FATHER-IN-LAW
Koado	TARŌ KAJA
3rd Ado	FRIEND OF THE GROOM

A new Groom on his way to his Father-in-law's house for his ceremonial first visit stops by to ask his Friend about the proper etiquette for the ceremony. His Friend (with the universal attitude towards newly married grooms) decides to tease him, so he says that the present-day popular method is to wear an extra-tall hat (which looks like a rooster's comb), and act like a rooster by crowing, and flapping one's arms like wings. When the Groom arrives at the Father-in-law's house, and begins performing in this manner, the Father-in-law immediately realizes what has happened, responds with the same, and the ceremony ends on a happy note with a song and dance.

NUKEGARA 脱殻
(Shedding the Demon Shell)

I O
和 大

Shite	TARŌ KAJA
Ado	MASTER

The Master calls Tarō Kaja, and orders him to go on an errand. It is his custom to give Tarō Kaja a drink of *saké* whenever he sends him on an errand, but he forgets this time. Tarō Kaja is determined to get his *saké*, and goes back several times on various pretenses till the Master finally realizes what is wrong.

Tarō Kaja, who is very fond of *saké*, gets drunk. He starts out on the errand, but on the way gets sleepy, and lies down beside the road for a nap. After some time has passed, the Master goes out to see what has happened, finds Tarō Kaja asleep, and decides to tease him a little. He puts a demon mask on Tarō Kaja, and goes back home to wait and see what will happen.

Tarō Kaja finally wakes up, remembers where he is and what he is supposed to be doing. He goes to a spring to wash the sleep out of his eyes, and is frightened by the demon he sees staring back at him. He decides to look once more to make sure it wasn't his imagination. This time he realizes it is himself, and begins to cry because he thinks he has turned into a demon. He goes to his Master's house. His Master pretends not to recognize him, and tries to chase him away. Tarō Kaja tries to convince the Master to use him in some way or other, but the Master says it is impossible to use a demon in his house.

Tarō Kaja decides there is nothing for him to do but die, so he goes back to the place he had been sleeping before, lies down, and the mask comes off. He picks up the mask, happily goes back to his Master, shows him the mask, and says that he has shed his demon shell. The Master scolds him for being so stupid.

In the Ōkura script, Tarō Kaja tries to jump in the well. As he jumps the mask comes off. The rest is the same as the Izumi script.

NURITSUKE 塗附 I
(Lacquered-While-You-Wait) 和

Shite	LACQUERER
Ado	DAIMYŌ I
Koado	DAIMYŌ II

It is the last day of the year and two Daimyōs are on their way to visit their parents. On the way they are discussing the fact that they both need to have their *eboshi* (a lacquered ceremonial tall hat) relacquered, when they meet a Lacquerer who claims to be the fastest lacquerer in the country. They tell him that they don't have time now, but early the next spring they want him to lacquer their *eboshi*s. The Lacquerer says that that's not necessary because his motto is service-while-you-wait. He even does the job without removing the hat from the head of the wearer. He says he also has a special system for drying the lacquer.

The Lacquerer runs a thread through both the hats, and ties them securely together, then puts a paper bag over both. When the bag is removed, the Daimyōs find they are stuck together. The Lacquerer has thus contrived to steal the hats. He puts a stick between them under the pretense of helping to pull them apart. As he pulls up, the hats become uncomfortable, so the Daimyōs both release the strings by which the hats are held on their heads. They realize, too late, that they have been tricked out of their hats.

NUSHI 塗師 (*See* Nushi Heiroku)

NUSHI HEIROKU 塗師平六
(Heiroku, the Lacquerer)

Shite	LACQUERER (HEIROKU)
Ado	MASTER LACQUERER (HEIROKU'S TEACHER)
Koado	WIFE (OF HEIROKU)

The Master Lacquerer, though he is a very skillful lacquerer, hasn't been having much business lately, so he decides to go visit a former student of his who lives in Echizen named Heiroku. He has heard that Heiroku, though he is quite unskillful, is very successful, and has more work than he can handle, so he hopes Heiroku will allow him to help with the work.

He reaches Echizen, and is heartily welcomed by Heiroku's Wife, but when she hears what he has come for, she fears for her Husband's business, since the only reason he is successful in the country is because there are no other lacquerers in the area. She decides she must somehow talk the Master into returning to the city. When the Master Lacquerer asks to see Heiroku, the Wife begins crying, and says that Heiroku died the previous autumn (In the Ōkura script, the Wife says that Heiroku died three years ago).

Heiroku, unaware of what is happening, comes into the room, and is very happy to see his old Teacher, but before he has had time for even a proper greeting, his Wife forces him out of the room, and tells him what has happened. They decide to dress Heiroku up as a ghost, and ask the Master Lacquerer to pray for his soul. The Master and the Wife go to the temple to pray for Heiroku's soul. Heiroku appears as a ghost to sing and dance in gratitude for their prayers.

NYAKUICHI 若市
(The Nun Nyakuichi's Revenge)

Shite	HEAD PRIEST
Ado	NYAKUICHI, A NUN
Koado	JŪKI, AN ACOLYTE
Tachishū	MANY NUNS

A young Nun named Nyakuichi is on her way to visit her home town with a bunch of flowers. She runs into the Head Priest, who is on his way back to the temple, and hides the flowers behind her back. The Head Priest scolds her for leaving the dormitory so often, accuses her of stealing the flowers from his garden, grabs the flowers and tears them to pieces, then beats Nyakuichi soundly.

Nyakuichi runs off crying, and the Head Priest continues on his way pleased with himself. Before long Jūki, an Acolyte, comes running to warn the Head Priest that Nyakuichi is coming to look for him followed by all the other Nuns, and that they are all in battle attire and looking very fierce.

The Head Priest and Jūki prepare themselves. Nyakuichi and the Nuns appear, and a very stylized fight ensues. This fight is in the form of song and dance, participated in by all. Nyakuichi finally knocks the Head Priest down, draws a razor and cuts off his hat.

Nyakuichi and the Nuns go off happily displaying the hat like a battle trophy.

In the Ōkura script, Nyakuichi and the Priest are not from the same temple, but just know each other. Also, Nyakuichi is on her way to visit another temple, not her home town. The Acolyte who comes to warn the Priest is not given a name. The rest is the same as the Izumi script.

OBA GA SAKÉ 伯母ケ酒

(The Stingy Aunt and her Saké)

I O

和 大

Shite   NEPHEW
Ado   AUNT

A Nephew goes to visit his stingy Aunt who owns a *saké* shop. She has never offered him even one sip of *saké*, so he is determined to talk her out of some this time. He tries many ways, but she refuses to the end. He starts home, and on the way decides to go back and trick her. He warns her that demons have been about recently in the evening, so she should keep her doors and windows tightly closed. This scares her to death, which assures him his plan will succeed.

The Nephew puts on a demon mask, and gets into his Aunt's house by pretending to be a customer. He threatens her with her life, and forces her to promise to be kinder to her Nephew in the future, then proceeds to help himself to her *saké*.

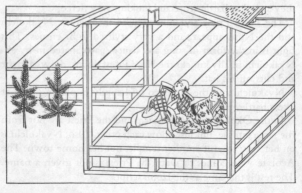

He begins drinking and finds the mask in the way. He warns her not to watch or he will eat her alive. As he gets progressively drunker, he shifts the mask to the side of his head, to his right hand, and finally to his knee, all the while threatening to eat her alive if she peeks in. Finally he drops off to sleep. The Aunt gathers enough courage to peek in, discovers the truth, and chases him off.

OCHA NO MIZU お茶の水 (*See* Mizu Kumi)

OHIYASHI お冷   I
(Wrapping Up Coolness)   和

> Shite   TARŌ KAJA
> Ado   MASTER

The heat is unbearable, so the Master calls Tarō Kaja and asks him where they could go to escape the heat. Tarō Kaja suggests going to the waterfall at Kiyomizu Temple.

When they reach the temple, the Master orders Tarō Kaja to go "wrap up some coolness" at which Tarō Kaja bursts out laughing. The Master retorts that all people of taste and fashion have always said "wrap up some coolness," but Tarō Kaja insists that the proper phrase is simply "draw water" which he proves by reciting a chanted narrative (*katari*) in which "draw water" is used. The Master answers with a song in which "wrap up some coolness" is used, but stops singing just before the last line, pretending he has forgotten it. Tarō Kaja sings the last line in which "draw water" is used. The Master chides him saying, "You could let your Master win an argument once in a while, don't you think?"

OKADAYŪ 岡太夫
(Rice Cakes Called Okadayū)

Shite	GROOM
Ado	FATHER-IN-LAW
Koado	TARŌ KAJA
Koado	WIFE (OF GROOM)

A Groom goes to his Father-in-law's house for his cere-monial first visit. Everying goes well, and after the ceremony, the Father-in-law serves some sweet rice cakes. The Groom likes them so well that he eats all of them and asks for more. Tarō Kaja explains that they are all gone, but the Father-in-law tells the Groom that his Wife knows how to make them, so he can have her make some as soon as he gets home. The Groom asks what they are called, and the Father-in-law explains that they are called *warabi mochi*. The Groom has a very poor memory and is afraid he won't be able to remember the name,

206

so the Father-in-law explains that there was an Emperor in ancient times who liked these rice cakes so much that he gave them court rank, and named them Okadayū, also that the name appears in a collection of poems that the Wife particularly likes to recite. The Groom feels sure he can remember at least one of these, so he rushes home and orders his Wife to cook this food for him. She doesn't know which food, and when he tries to explain, the only thing he can remember is the collection of poems.

The Wife recites several poems, but finally loses patience. The Groom gets angry at her impudence, and begins to beat her. In her plea for mercy, she inadvertently recites the correct poem. They are both happy the problem is solved, and the Wife offers to make him some Okadayū immediately.

OKO SAKO 右近左近 (*See* Uchizata)

ONGYOKU MUKO 音曲聟
(The Rhythmical Groom)

I
和

Shite	GROOM
Ado	FATHER-IN-LAW
Koado	TARŌ KAJA
Koado	FRIEND (OF GROOM)

A new Groom on his was to pay his ceremonial first visit to his Father-in-law stops by a Friend's house to ask for instructions in the proper way to carry out the ceremony. The Friend takes advantage of the Groom's innocence, and tells him that all that is necessary when he is presented to his Father-in-law

is to walk three steps forward, three steps backward, whirl around twice and sit down. Also, everything he says should be spoken to a rhythm.

The Father-in-law at first thinks the Groom is crazy, but soon realizes what has happened. He plays along with the gag by putting all his own words to a rhythm. The ceremony ends happily with singing and dancing.

ONIGAWARA 鬼瓦
(The Demon-Faced Tile)

I O
和 大

Shite	DAIMYŌ
Ado	TARŌ KAJA

A Daimyō who has been in the capital on business for a long time, has just received permission to return home, and is very happy. He calls Tarō Kaja and tells him the news. Tarō Kaja suggests that they go pay their respects at the temple before they leave.

The Daimyō wants to build a similar temple at home, so he and Tarō Kaja take special note of how the temple is constructed so they can tell the carpenters exactly what they want. They are looking at the outside of the temple when suddenly the Daimyō begins weeping. Tarō Kaja asks him what the matter is, and he points to the demon-faced end tile (similar to the gargoyles on the roofs of medieval cathedrals), and says that the face reminds him of his wife and has made him homesick. He points out how each horrible feature is exactly the same as his wife's, becoming more and more maudlin. Finally Tarō Kaja reminds him that they will soon be going home, and he will be able to see his wife, so there is no reason to carry on so. The Daimyō agrees that he should be laughing instead of crying, invites Tarō Kaja to laugh with him, and they go off together laughing heartily.

ONIMARU 鬼丸 (Onimaru Reforms) 和

Mae Shite	PRIEST
Ato Shite	KANNON (SOMETIMES CALLED THE GODdess of Mercy)
Ado	ONIMARU
Koado	GRANDFATHER

A Priest is travelling along the road and gets tired, so he asks for lodging at the Grandfather's house. The Grandfather, a very kind old man, grants his request, and shows him to his room. They chat for a while during which the Grandfather reveals that he is a worshipper of Kannon, and that he has a son named Onimaru who takes good care of him.

They say good night, and the Priest sleeps for a while. He wakes up while it is still dark, and not wanting to disturb his host, leaves quietly.

Onimaru, the Grandfather's son, is actually a highway robber. He stops the Priest, and demands his possessions or his life. The Priest gives him all he has, and also tells him of the evils and consequences of robbery, even when it is for a good cause. Onimaru repents, and the Priest disappears without receiving his things back.

Onimaru goes home still dressed as a highway robber, and confesses what he has done, and tells about the Priest. The Grandfather is very angry, grabs Onimaru's halberd, and is frantically chasing after him threatening to kill him, when the Priest appears again, this time in the form of Kannon. He charges the Grandfather to forgive Onimaru, and Onimaru to prove his repentance by becoming a priest.

ONI NO MAMAKO 鬼の継子   I O
(The Demon's Stepchild)   和 大

Shite　DEMON
Ado　WOMAN

A Woman, whose husband Saburō Tōgo died the previous year, has found it too hard to support herself and her baby, and has decided to go home to her parents. On the way she comes to a very lonely place in the road at about dusk. Suddenly a Demon jumps out, and threatens to eat her. She explains who she is, and begs for her life. The Demon says he knows her

210

husband because it is his duty to torture Saburō Tōgo in hell. The Woman asks about her husband, and pleads with the Demon to intercede with Emma, the King of Hell, to have Saburō Tōgo sent to heaven. The Demon agrees on the condition that she will become his wife. She is reluctant at first, but finally agrees. He says she can't go with him as she is, and orders her to dry her tears, and make herself pretty. She gives him the baby to hold while she fixes herself up. At first he thinks the baby looks very tasty, but she reminds him it is now his own child. He begins to act like a human being, and plays with the child, but finally decides it is too tasty looking a morsel to miss, gets ready to eat it, and the Woman runs off crying for help.

In the Ōkura script, no mention is made of the Woman's husband (except for the fact that she had been married). She agrees to marry the Demon to save her baby's life and her own. The rest is the same as the Izumi script.

ORIGAMI MUKO 折紙聟
(The Dowery of Paper Toys)

Shite	GROOM
Ado	FATHER-IN-LAW
Koado	TARŌ KAJA
3rd Ado	WOMAN (WIFE OF GROOM)

A newly married Groom takes his Wife along for his ceremonial first visit to the Father-in-law's house. This visit is for the purpose of receiving the Father-in-law's blessing and the dowry. The Groom has been promised a gold sword and a large amount of money, but is only presented with the ceremonial blessings and plenty of *saké*. He gets disgusted and leaves. His Wife follows quickly, and asks him what is wrong. He retorts that he has been cheated by her and her Father, and that he wants a divorce. She finally soothes him by presenting him with some folded paper toys (*origami*) in token of the promised dowry. She explains that the sword shop is very busy, and hasn't been able to finish his sword yet, but as soon as it is finished, it will be delivered to him along with the promised money. He sings his apology, and they start towards home happily.

ŌTŌNAI 大藤内 (Ōtōnai, the Sissy)

| Shite | ŌTŌNAI |
| Ado | PASSER-BY |

A Priest named Ōtōnai, dressed in girl's clothes, runs on

screaming and whimpering. A Passer-by asks him what is wrong, and he explains that he is just a poor little priest, come in from the country to take care of some business, and soon after he reached the city, he met this nice man named Kudō Zaemon Tsuketsune, and since that time, dear Tsuketsune has just been so nice, letting him stay at his house and all. And he goes on to say that until a little while ago, they were just having this nice party, and everyone had settled down for the night, when suddenly some awful sounds came from the next room, and just as he got up and peeked through the door, this big man came at him with a sword, and he was so scared that he ran all this way.

The Passer-by asks if he is hurt, but he says he doesn't think so, but that he is so very scared. The Passer-by realizes he is just a silly girlish coward, and decides to give him a good teasing. He tells him that his back is split wide open, whereupon Ōtōnai screams in pain, but dries his tears again as soon as he is told it was just a joke. The Passer-by asks him why he is dressed in girl's clothes, and he explains that a few of them were just having a little fun, and he hadn't had time to change.

The Passer-by, tired of Ōtōnai's hysterics, tells him that the man he has been staying with is probably dead by now because he was the enemy of the Soga Brothers, and that he can see one of them coming this way with his sword drawn right now. Ōtōnai begins crying again, and clings to the Passer-by. The Passer-by knocks him down, says, "Get your hands off me, you silly sissy!" and leaves completely disgusted.

RAKUAMI 楽阿弥
(Rakuami, the Flute Playing Priest)

I O
和 大

Shite	GHOST OF RAKUAMI
Waki	TRAVELLING PRIEST
Ai	VILLAGER

A Travelling Priest on a pilgrimage to the Grand Shrine of Ise comes to a place called Matsubara in Beppō. He sees a large pine tree on which are hung many *shakuhachi* (a kind of Japanese flute), and since he himself is very fond of playing the *shakuhachi*, he asks a passing Villager the reason for this tree covered with *shakuhachi*.

The Villager explains that many years ago a priest named Rakuami who loved to play the *shakuhachi* had lived and died in this place. He was buried under this tree, and it has since become a custom for those who come to pray for his soul to hang a *shakuhachi* on the tree as a memorial.

The Priest prays for Rakuami, and begins to play a piece on his *shakuhachi*. The Ghost of Rakuami appears, having been awakened by the sound of the *shakuhachi*. Rakuami thanks the Priest for his prayer and music. They play together, then Rakuami dances, and tells of his life in a song, then disappears.

This is a Nō-gakari Kyōgen which means it was constructed in the Noh style.

RENGA JITTOKU 連歌十徳
(A Poem or a Robe?)

I
和

Shite	HUSBAND
Ado	RICH MAN

| Ado | WIFE |
| Ado | PRIEST |

A Rich Man puts up a sign advertising for a priest who knows the ten rules (*jittoku*) of *renga* (a kind of linked poem).

A Wife chases her Husband out with a stick, and threatens him with his life if he doesn't go out and make some money since he has gambled away not only all their money, but all their movable possessions as well.

The Husband goes to see a Priest for advice. The Priest tells him of the Rich Man who is offering ten *kan* for a priest. The Husband agrees to disguise himself. The Priest gives him a priest's robe (also pronouced *jittoku*), which he says is the necessary "*Renga* Robe," and shaves his head for him.

The Husband goes to the Rich Man's house, and finds that the ten *kan* is not money, but ten rolls of seaweed. He starts to leave in a huff. The Rich Man grabs him, and the Husband complains that the precious *Renga* Robe will be torn. The Rich Man realizes he has been tricked, and chases him off.

RENGA NUSUBITO　連歌盗人　　I　O
(The Poem Loving Thieves)　　　　和　大

Shite	THIEF I
Ado	THIEF II
Koado	RICH NEIGHBOR

Two poor Men are to be hosts for the next *renga* (a kind of linked poem) meeting. They don't have the proper equipment or the money to buy it with, so they decide to steal these things from a rich neighbor. They break into his house, but instead

of stealing the equipment and running away, they find the
first line of a poem written on a poem card, and begin to compose poems and sing them.

They are caught, but instead of treating them like thieves,
the Neighbor, also a great lover of *renga*, insists that they
continue poem making in which he joins them, serves them
saké, and finally presents them with the equipment they came
to steal, and sends them happily home with an open invitation
to come back any time.

ROKU JIZŌ 六地蔵
(The Six Statues)

Shite	SHYSTER	
Ado	COUNTRY MAN	
Tachishū	FRIENDS OF SHYSTER	

216

A Country Man goes to the capital to buy six statues of the Buddhist God Jizō for a new temple he and his fellow villagers have built, but when he arrives, he remembers that he doesn't know where a sculptor lives or what one looks like, so he decides to shout as he walks along the streets that he wants to find a sculptor and buy six statues of Jizō. A Shyster hears the Country Man, and decides to trick him out of his money. He claims that he is the only true living Sculptor of a long line of famous sculptors.

The Shyster asks what kinds of Jizō the Country Man desires, and he explains what sacred tools they should be holding, and what positions they should be in. The Country Man asks when they will be finished. The Shyster says it will take three years, three months, and ninety days. The Country Man asks if they can't be finished a little sooner to which the Shyster replies that if he is in a hurry, they can be finished the next day. If he makes them himself, it will take three years, three months, and ninety days, but if he has his students do it, they can be finished by the

217

next day at the same time. They decide on the price and the place for the statues to be received, and part till the next day.

The Shyster calls on his friends to help him, and has them pose as the statues, but since there are only three of them, they decide to only show the Country Man three at a time, and have the other three in a different place. Thus they will each pose as two different statues. They prepare themselves with costumes, masks, sacred tools, etc., and pose for the showing of the first three statues.

The Country Man appears at the appointed time, sees the first three statues, and is quite happy with them, but wants some minor adjustments made. He calls the Shyster to order changes and ask about the remaining three. The Shyster explains that they were too big to put all six in one place, so the rest of them are near the temple bell.

The Country Man is pleased with these also, but again wants minor changes made. He goes back and forth so many times to check on the changes and to order more, that finally the three posing as statues get so confused in their quick changes, that they get the masks on crooked, the tools upside down, the poses wrong, and finally even bump into the Country Man on the trip from one place to the other. The Country Man realizes what has happened and chases them all off.

In the Ōkura script, the Shyster says he can have the statues done either the next day at the same time or the next year at the same time. The Shyster has only two Friends to help him, so he is very busy. In the end, he gets so confused that he tries to set the Country Man up as a statue. The rest is the same as the Izumi script.

ROKUNINSŌ 六人僧 (Six Shaved Heads)

Shite	MAN I
Ado	MAN II
Koado	MAN III
Koado	WIFE II
Koado	WIFE III
Koado	WIFE I

Three Friends start out on a pilgrimage together. They swear to each other not to get angry under any circumstances during the course of this holy trip. They have been travelling for some time, when Man I says he is sleepy, and suggests they stop for a rest. He lies down and is sound asleep immediately, but the other two cannot seem to get to sleep, and hard as they try, they can't wake Man I up. Man II suggests that they shave Man I's head and dress him as a priest. Man III is reluctant, but finally agrees to help.

219

When Man I wakes up, and discovers what has happened, he gets angry and accuses the other two of doing it. They, of course, pretend innocence, and remind him that no matter who did what, they have all made a vow not to get angry. Man I says he can't continue on the trip looking like this, tells them good-bye, and heads for home. Man II and Man III continue blithely on their way.

When Man I reaches their home town, he immediately goes to the Wives of the other two, tells them their Husbands drowned as they were crossing a river, and that he has become a priest to pray for their souls. The Women are very sad and want to commit suicide, but he convinces them to become Nuns, and join him in praying for their Husbands' souls. They agree, he shaves their heads for them, and leaves again saying he will take their hair to Mt. Kōya and perform the final rites for their dedication as Nuns.

Man I meets Man II and Man III on the road as he had expected, and tells them that when he got home, some prankster had spread the rumor that the three of them hadn't gone on a pilgrimage at all, but had gone to the capital with three other women, and were having a good time instead. He says that his own Wife went to the capital in a fit of rage to find him, but the other two Wives went crazy with jealousy, and died swearing to haunt their husbands.

Man II and Man III think Man I is only trying to get back at them, and refuse to believe his story till he shows them their Wives' hair at the sight of which they are scared out of their wits, and beg Man I for advice. He advises them to take the tonsure at once, and spend the rest of their lives praying for their Wives' forgiveness, and peaceful rest for their souls. They agree, and he shaves their heads for them. Then they all three start toward home to pray for the souls of the two dead Wives.

When they reach the temple in their home town, they run into the two Wives who have come to recite their sutras. Man II, Man III and their Wives realize what has happened and are angry, but Man I reminds them that they have all sworn that they would not get angry. The Four decide to go find Man I's Wife and shave her head too. They are about to leave to carry out this plan when she appears dressed as a nun with her head already shaved.

She explains that she has heard all that has happened, and decided to join the rest, of her own free will. Then she suggests that they all repent of their sins and pray for life after death, the three Women in a nunnery, and the three Men on the pilgrimage they had originally planned. They all agree and sing together a song about the sadness of parting, and the happiness of life after death.

RŌMUSHA 老武者
(The Old Men Win the Boy)

和 大

Shite	GRANDFATHER
Ado	CHILD
Koado	SANI (A NOBLEMAN)
3rd Ado	INNKEEPER
Tachishū	SEVERAL YOUNG MEN
Musha Tachishū	SEVERAL OLD MEN

Sani has brought a beautiful Child of noble birth to see Kamakura. They are travelling incognito so as not to attract attention, but the word has gotten around, and a group of Young Men come to the inn where they are staying to see the Child and have a few drinks with him. The Innkeeper tries to keep them out, but they force their way in. They are all drinking, singing, and dancing together when the oldest Grandfather in the town comes to see the Child. The Innkeeper says this is a party for young people, and tries to send him home, but he insists on going in. One of the Young Men comes out, then Sani comes out, and they finally throw the old Man out bodily and shut the door in his face. He goes off very angry, and comes back very soon with many other old Men armed with halberds and javelins. The Young Men and the Old Men fight. The Old Men win, and go off triumphantly with the Child on their shoulders. Sani thinks it rather strange that all these Men should make such a fuss over a young boy.

In the Ōkura script, when the Old Men come back prepared to fight, the Young Men laugh at them for trying to be warriors at their age. The Old Men remind them that many famous warriors fought at the age of seventy or even eighty. The Young Men finally quiet the Old Men down and all go off toward home together.

ROREN 呂連 (Almost a Priest) I O 和 大

Shite	PRIEST
Ado	TEA SHOP OWNER
Koado	WIFE OF TEA SHOP OWNER

A Travelling Priest requests lodging for the night at a tea shop. The Owner invites him in, and while they are waiting for the evening meal to be prepared, the Owner asks questions about heaven, hell, and life after death. Then he asks the Priest to shave his head and make him a priest. The Priest is very happy to perform the rites, but first asks the Owner if he has

the permission of his Wife and family. The Owner assures him there is nothing to worry about, so the Priest shaves his head.

When this is done, the Owner asks the Priest to give him a new name. The Priest has never given anyone a new name before, so he finally decides to use his alphabet book. The Owner says that one of the letters of the name must be *ren*. The Priest begins going through the alphabet, and finds this Owner become priest very hard to please, but the name Roren is finally decided upon.

At this point the Wife of the Owner appears to announce that supper is ready. When she discovers what has happened, she becomes angry. The Owner says the Priest forced him to do it, so the Wife scolds the Priest. The Priest, of course, refuses to take the responsibility, but the Wife believes her Husband. They join forces and throw the Priest down, beat him, and go off together. The Priest gets up, dusts himself off, and says, "If this is what one has to go through to make a new convert, I shall never try it again!"

223

In the Ōkura script, the Owner says the Priest forced him to become a priest, then he leaves. The Wife demands that the Priest give her Husband back his hair. The Priest says it will grow back naturally in two or three years. The Wife chases the Priest off scolding. The rest is the same as the Izumi script.

SADOGITSUNE 佐渡狐 (The Sado Fox) I O
和 大

Shite	FARMER FROM SADO
Ado	FARMER FROM ECHIGO
Koado	TAX COLLECTOR

A Farmer from Sado and a Farmer from Echigo meet on the way to the capital to pay their taxes, and decide to travel together. As they are going along, they chat about various things. The Farmer from Echigo says that it must be very inconvenient to live in Sado for he has heard that since Sado is an

island, there are many things that aren't available there.

The Farmer from Sado is highly insulted, and claims that there is absolutely nothing that is not available in Sado. The Farmer from Echigo says he is sure there are no foxes in Sado. The Farmer from Sado is caught, but rather than admit defeat, he stubbornly maintains that there are foxes in Sado. They bet their swords on it, and decide to have the Tax Collector arbitrate for them.

When they reach the capital, the Farmer from Sado goes in to see the Tax Collector first. After he has paid his taxes, he tells the Tax Collector about their wager, and bribes him. The Tax Collector teaches him how to describe a fox.

The Echigo Farmer pays his taxes, then presents his case to the Tax Collector who immediately decides in favor of the Sado Farmer. The Echigo Farmer, as was expected, asks for a description of a fox. The Sado Farmer gets confused and forgets everything, but the Tax Collector, using frantic gestures and grimaces, finally gets it all across to him. The Sado Farmer receives the two swords, and the two Farmers leave.

After they get outside, the Echigo Farmer suddenly realizes that he forgot to ask for the cry of the fox. The Sado Farmer responds with the description he had been taught previously. The Echigo Farmer persistently demands the cry of the fox. Finally in desperation, the Sado Farmer gives the call of the nightingale. The Echigo Farmer grabs the swords, and runs off with the Sado Farmer close at his heels pleading, "At least let me have my own sword back!"

In the Ōkura script, the Sado Farmer give a rooster's crow instead of the nightingale's song for the cry of the fox. The rest is the same as the Izumi script.

SAIHŌ 財宝 (Three Grandsons Named)　　I　O
和　大

Shite	GRANDFATHER (SAIHŌ)
Ado	GRANDSON I
Koado	GRANDSON II
3rd Ado	GRANDSON III

Three Grandsons have reached the age to be given names, so they go to ask their wealthy, but stingy Grandfather to pick names for them. When they arrive, the Grandfather, whose eyesight is failing, still thinks of them as young children, and gives them each a toy as a gift. They remind him that they have grown up, and tell him that they have come to receive their adult names from him. This makes him very happy, and he gives them names that are appropriate to their personalities. They all drink and sing and dance in celebration. Finally they make a chair of their arms, and carry their Grandfather off, all singing happily.

In the Ōkura script, the Grandfather does not mistake the Grandsons for children. He scolds them for not receiving names from their parents.

On particularly felicitous occasions, the Ōkura school performs this Kyōgen as a Waki Kyōgen in which case there is no mention of the Grandfather's stinginess, and there is no drinking and dancing. Otherwise it is the same as the Izumi script.

SAI NO ME 賽の目 (Counting Dice Spots)　　I
和

Shite	GROOM I

226

Ado	RICH MAN
Koado	TARŌ KAJA
Koado	GROOM II
Koado	GROOM III
Koado	OTSU (DAUGHTER OF RICH MAN)

A Rich Man advertises that he will give Otsu, his only daughter, in marriage to anyone who is good at mathematics. Groom II appears, and the Rich Man asks him how many spots are on five hundred dice. The Groom begins to try to find the answer by counting on his fingers. The Rich Man sees this, and sends him away. Groom III appears, and when he is asked the same question, asks for paper and pencil to figure out the answer. He is also sent away.

Groom I appears, and informs the Rich Man that he is the best mathematician in Japan. The Rich Man asks him the same question, and Groom I answers immediately with the correct answer. The Rich Man is very pleased, and leaves Groom I and Otsu alone together.

They promise each other to live happily together forever, but when Otsu takes off her veil, her face is so ugly that the Groom says, "No amount of money would convince me to marry a face like that!" And he runs off followed closely by Otsu crying, "But you promised! Wait for me!"

SAKEKŌ NO SHIKI 酒講式
(A Parent–Teacher Problem)

和

Shite   TEACHER
Ado   PARENT OF PUPIL

The Parent of one of the pupils goes to visit the Teacher, because his son has been hurt. It looks like he has been beaten with a bamboo stick. The Teacher is a well-known lover of *saké*, so the Parent takes along some *saké* as a gift. The Teacher explains that the boys have been playing in the bushes lately, and that is probably how the son was hurt.

The Teacher suggests that they drink together, but the parent refuses saying that he doesn't drink. The Teacher drinks all the *saké* by himself, gets quite drunk, and tries to convince the Parent that *saké* is good for the body and soul. The Parent finally gets disgusted, and says that he will tell the whole village what a drunkard the Teacher is, and see that no one sends their children to his school. The Teacher answers that he doesn't care if he doesn't have any pupils as long as he has *saké*. The Parent gets even angrier at this, and chases the drunken Teacher off. (Two or more Parents are sometimes used.)

SAKKA 咲嘩 (Sakka, the Thief)

I
和

Shite	TARŌ KAJA
Ado	MASTER
Koado	SAKKA

The Master sends Tarō Kaja to the capital to invite the Master's uncle to come and help him teach *renga* (a kind of linked poem).

When Tarō Kaja reaches the capital, he remembers that he doesn't know the uncle's name, what he looks like, or where he lives, so he begins to shout that he wants to find his Master's uncle. A famous thief named Sakka says he is the uncle, and they go home together.

The Master recognizes Sakka, but doesn't want to make an enemy of him, so he tells Tarō Kaja to entertain him till the meal is ready. Tarō Kaja makes all kinds of mistakes in etiquette, till the Master instructs him to do and say just as he does. Tarō Kaja begins to parrot the Master's words and actions. The Master gets angry, and begins to beat Tarō Kaja who in turn beats Sakka. The Master finally throws Tarō Kaja down and goes off. Tarō Kaja throws Sakka down, and follows his Master off. Sakka gets up, brushes himself off, and goes off in a daze.

SAKO NO SAMURŌ 左近三郎
(The Hunter and the Priest)

O
大

Shite	SAKO NO SAMURŌ
Ado	PRIEST

229

Sako no Samurō, the Hunter, goes out hunting. He meets a Priest on the road, and decides to tease him. Samurō forces the Priest to admit that he eats fish and was once married. When the Priest finds out that Samurō is a hunter, he begins quoting scriptures to show him he will go to hell if he continues to kill living things. Samurō misquotes several passages trying to prove the opposite. The Priest tells him there is a passage which says, if you kill a deer, you will become a deer. Samurō laughs, aims at the Priest, and says, "Well then, if I kill you, I will become a priest."

The Priest explains that Samurō must not kill him because he has a Buddha in his heart. Samurō says he will cut open the Priest's breast, so he can see the Buddha. The Priest tells the story of the man who split open a cherry tree to see the blossoms which are said to be in the heart of every cherry tree, and found nothing there. Samurō says, "But there was a blossom" (the words for "nose" and "blossom" are both *hana* in Japanese). The Priest asks where, and Samurō says, "In the middle of your face." They both have a good laugh and go off together in a merry mood.

SANBONBASHIRA 三本柱
(Three Poles)

Shite	WEALTHY MAN
Ado	TARŌ KAJA
Koado	JIRŌ KAJA
3rd Ado	SABURŌ KAJA

A Wealthy Man calls his three Servants, and orders them to go to the mountain and bring back three poles, and each of them is to carry two poles each. They go get the poles, and begin carrying one apiece, which they find very heavy. One of them remembers what the Master said about each one carrying two poles, so they stop to rest and think how to carry two apiece. They happen to sit down in a triangle, and suddenly they realize that if they each take the end of two poles, thus forming a triangle, they will each be carrying two poles. They continue on their was home in this manner singing and dancing. When they reach home, the Master dances with them, then rewards them for their cleverness.

SANBON NO HASHIRA 三本の柱
(*See* Sanbonbashira)

SANNINBU 三人夫 (Three Farmers)

Shite	FARMER FROM MINO
Ado	FARMER FROM AWAJI
Koado	FARMER FROM OWARI
Koado	TAX COLLECTOR

A Farmer from Mino, one from Awaji, and one from Owari go together to pay their taxes. The Tax Collector orders them each to compose a part of a poem using the name of their own region. Then he serves them drinks, and asks them their names. He makes fun of their names, and orders them to make a poem using their names. They all drink more, and go off singing and dancing together in celebration.

SANNIN CHŌJA 三人長者
(Three Millionaires)

Shite	SESENAGI, A MILLIONAIRE FROM KŌCHI
Ado	GAMŌ, A MILLIONAIRE FROM ŌMI
Koado	ICHIMORI, A MILLIONAIRE FROM YAMATO

Three millionaires meet on their way home from being given official names in the capital. They decide to celebrate the receiving of their new names before continuing on their way home. Each tells the story of how his name was chosen. Then they begin to drink and sing and dance. Finally each announces his own name, and they all happily set out on their separate ways home.

232

SANNIN KATAWA 三人片輪
(The Handicapped Three)

Shite	MUTE
Ado	WEALTHY MAN
Koado	BLIND MAN
3rd Ado	CRIPPLE

A Wealthy Man advertises that he wants to hire handicapped servants. One man who has lost everything gambling pretends to be blind, and is hired. Another in the same circumstances pretends to be a cripple who has lost the use of both legs, and is hired. A Third pretends to be a mute, and is hired.

The Wealthy Man puts the Blind Man in charge of the linen closets, the Cripple in charge of the Wine Cellar, and the Mute in charge of the Safe, then goes out on some business or other.

The Three have come separately, been interviewed, and hired in separate rooms, so have not seen each other. They are all curious about who else has come. They all get together and discover that they are old friends and gambling partners. They decide to open the wine cellar, have a few drinks, then open the safe and do some gambling.

The drinking party is in full swing with singing and dancing when the Wealthy Man returns and discovers them. In the confusion, each picks up the wrong equipment for his handicap. The Wealthy Man chases them all off grumbling about the trick that has been played on him.

233

SARU MUKO　猿聟　　　　　　I
(The Monkey Groom)　　　　　和

Shite	MONKEY GROOM
Ado	MONKEY FATHER-IN-LAW
Tachishū	MONKEY SERVANTS, AND MEMBERS OF THE THE MONKEY FAMILY

A Monkey Groom goes to make his ceremonial first visit to his Monkey Father-in-law who lives on Arashiyama. Most of the dialogue is in monkey chatter which is expressed by *kya kya* in Japanese. The ceremony is performed, *saké* is served, and everyone drinks, sings, and dances in celebration of the happy occasion.

SARU ZATŌ　猿座頭　　　　I　O
(The Blind Man and the Monkey)　和　大

Shite	BLIND MAN
Ado	WIFE OF BLIND MAN
Koado	MONKEY TRAINER
Koado	MONKEY

A Blind Man takes his Wife out flower viewing saying that since he can't see the flowers, he will enjoy them by smelling them. They reach the Kiyomizu Temple, and are drinking and singing to each other.

A Monkey Trainer, attracted first by the Wife's voice, decides to take her away from the Blind Man, as soon as he sees her face is as attractive as her voice. The Wife, tired of wasting her youth tied to a blind man, is easily convinced to go with

234

the handsome Monkey Trainer, but the Blind Man keeps calling her back, and scolding her for not staying by his side. Finally the Blind Man ties a cord around her waist so she can't get away. This makes the Wife angry, and strengthens her desire to leave the Blind Man.

The Monkey Trainer unties the Wife, and ties his Monkey to the cord instead while the Blind Man is singing a song, then they go off happily together.

When the Blind Man finishes his song and gets no response from his Wife, he pulls the cord. The Monkey jumps on him and scratches his face. The Blind Man thinks his Wife has turned into a Monkey, and runs off crying for help with the Monkey clinging to his back.

SATSUMANOKAMI 薩摩守
(The Forgotten Boat Fare)

I O
和 大

Shite	TRAVELLING PRIEST
Ado	TEA SHOP OWNER
Koado	BOATMAN

A Travelling Priest goes along the road, and just when he is feeling thirsty, the Tea Shop Owner calls to him to come in and have a cup of tea. The Priest drinks his tea and when it comes time to pay, he admits that he has no money. The Owner feels sorry for him, and not only gives him the tea free, but tells him that there is a river close by that he will have to cross by ferry boat. and if he doesn't pay the fare in the middle of the river, he won't be able to get across. The Owner also tells the Priest that the Boatman is very fond of *shūku*, a kind of riddle, and teaches him one which he says can be used in place of the boat fare. The riddle consists of using a name that contains the sound *tadanori* which also means free ride.

The Priest reaches the river, and calls for the Boatman, but the Boatman will not come for only one person, so the Priest lies and says that he is with a large group that will be along presently, and that he must go ahead to arrange for lodging for the night.

The Boatman lets him aboard at this, and in the middle of the river asks for the fare. The Priest recites the first line of the riddle. The Boatman is happily surprised, and asks how the Priest knew he liked *shūku*. The Priest replies that the Boatman is famous all over the country for his fondness of *shūku*. This makes the Boatman so happy that he invites the Priest to stay at his house for five or ten days, and he will personally see the Priest to his destination.

The Boatman wants to hear the punch line of the *shūku*, but since the Priest has forgotten what it was, he says that he will tell it after the boat reaches the shore. When the boat reaches the shore, he gets off, and says he will tell it on his way home. At this the Boatman loses all patience, and chases the Priest off.

In the Ōkura script, the Priest finally recalls an answer, but it is the wrong answer. The rest is the same as the Izumi script.

SEIRAI　政頼　　　　　　　　I O
(Seirai, the Hawk Keeper and Emma,　　和 大
the King of Hell)

Shite	SEIRAI, THE HAWK KEEPER
Ado	EMMA, THE KING OF HELL
Tachishū	DEMONS
Tachishū	DOGS

236

Emma, the King of Hell, has come upon hard days as a result of all the new religions which help sinners get to heaven. Things have gotten so bad that he has brought some Demons and come to the Crossing of the Six Roads to catch sinners and chase them to Hell.

Seirai, a Hawk Keeper, comes along and is captured by the Demons, and brought before Emma. He explains how hawks are used to catch birds, and that this is a sport participated in only by the highest nobility. He tells the history of hawks in a chanted narrative (*katari*).

Emma is fascinated, and asks for a demonstration. The Demons are used as beaters, and Emma is the lord of the hunt. Emma is so happy with the delicous birds that he promises to grant one wish for Seirai. Seirai wishes to return to the world of the living. Emma reluctantly grants him three years of life, on the condition that Seirai will send him plenty of tasty birds to eat during that time. Emma makes Seirai a present of his crown, and Seirai goes happily back to the world of the living.

237

SEMI 蟬 (The Locust)

Shite	LOCUST
Waki	PRIEST
Ai	VILLAGER

A Priest comes to a beautiful pine tree on his way to the Zen-kō Temple in Shinano, and decides to rest under its branches. When he comes closer, he notices a poem card on one of its branches, reads it, and finds it expresses sadness in parting with a Locust. Thinking this strange, he asks a passing Villager about it.

The Villager explains that in the summer, the villagers always gather under this tree to sing songs and compose poems while viewing the pine tree and listening to the locusts. The previous year an especially large Locust came, but was soon eaten by the crows. Because of its size, the people believe that the Locust had a soul, so when they pass this tree, they pray for its soul, and tie poem cards to the branches of the tree in memory of the Locust.

The Priest is praying for the soul of the Locust when its ghost appears before him and thanks him for his prayers. The Ghost of the Locust tells in a song and dance of his death, and of his experiences in the other world.

This Kyōgen is a Nōgakari, meaning it is composed in the form of a Noh Drama, but handles lighter Kyōgen-type material.

SENJIMONO 煎じ物 (The Tea Seller)

Shite MEDICINAL TEA SELLER

Ado   HEAD OF FESTIVAL FLOAT COMMITTEE
Koado   TARŌ KAJA
Tachishū   MUSICIANS

It is nearly time for the annual festival, so the Head of the
Festival Float Committee sends Tarō Kaja to call the Musicians
in order to rehearse the song and dance to be performed on the
float. They all gather at the Head's house and begin their
rehearsal.

A Medicinal Tea Seller appears, and begins to try to sell his
tea. The Musicians all refuse, but he persists till he almost
completely disrupts the rehearsal. The Head finally explains
to him that if he will do his sales-talk in time with the music,
all will go well. The Tea Seller complies, and all goes well and
fits into the rhythm, the tea selling, the singing of both the
Musicians and the Tea Seller, and the drinking of the tea.

The Head adds his dance to the song. The dance is performed
with a small drum tied to the front of his waist which he strikes
as he dances. The Tea Seller becomes so interested in the dance,

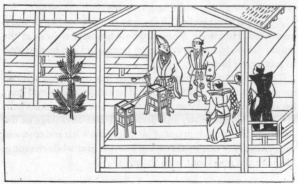

that he forgets about his tea, and begins dancing with the Head. The Tea Seller finally ties one of his earthern ware pots to his waist in place of the drum. The dance ends by turning cart wheels off the stage which the Tea Seller tries and falls on his pot.

If the pot actually breaks, he says, "What good luck, I had only one, but now I have many!" If the pot doesn't break, he says, "What good luck to have such a strong, well-made pot!"

SETSUBUN 節分 (A Demon in Love)　　Ｉ　Ｏ
　　　　　　　　　　　　　　　　　　　　　　　　　　和　大

| Shite | DEMON |
| Ado | WOMAN |

This Kyōgen is closely connected with the Spring holiday of the same name at which time demons and bad spirits are driven out of the house by scattering red beans in all the rooms while chanting, "In with the good, out with the evil."

A Demon has travelled all the way from Hōrai Island, and is very tired. He asks a Woman whose husband is away at the Izumo Shrine to let him rest in her house, and she, being afraid to refuse, lets him in.

The Demon tries to make love to her by singing various songs praising her beauty, etc., and he finally breaks into tears because she won't pay any attention to him. She realizes he is just like a human male, and decides to take advantage of the situation. She tricks him out of his magic straw hat and coat, and then chases him out by throwing beans at him while chanting, "In with the good, out with the evil!"

SHATEI 舎弟 (The Brother Fight)　　I　O
和　大

Shite	YOUNGER BROTHER
Ado	FRIEND
Koado	OLDER BROTHER

Whenever Younger Brother goes to visit his Older Brother, Older Brother always calls him Shatei instead of his given name. Younger Brother doesn't know the meaning of Shatei, so he goes to consult a Friend of his. The Friend decides to have some fun with Younger Brother, and tells him that Shatei means "thief."

Younger Brother goes to Older Brother's house in a rage. Older Brother greets him as usual, and is mystified when Younger Brother shouts back, "What do you mean calling people names?" Older Brother laughingly explains that Shatei is simply a familiar term meaning younger brother. Younger Brother, still convinced that his Friend had told him the truth, says, "You are the thief in the family. I remember a couple of years ago when you stole a white cow from one village, painted it black, and sold it in another village." Older Brother responds, "You're not so faultless yourself. I remember last year when you stole rice plants from another field to plant in your own." Younger Brother comes back with, "What about the tea cup you stole at the party here while back?" Older Brother claims he didn't steal it, but it was given to him. Younger Brother says, "Then why did you have to give it back?"

Older Brother grabs Younger Brother, and throws him down, saying, "This will teach you!" Younger Brother gets up, throws Older Brother down, and runs off gleefully shouting, "I won! I won!" Older Brother slowly picks himself up grumbling, "You'll have a black future if you don't learn to respect your elders!"

The only difference in the Ōkura script is that the Older Brother doesn't accuse the Younger Brother of stealing, and the Younger Brother's accusations are in the opposite order.

SHIBIRI しびり (Inherited Cramps)
和 大 I O

Shite	TARŌ KAJA
Ado	MASTER

The Master orders Tarō Kaja to go to Izumi to buy provisions, because the neighborhood shops don't have very good wares. Tarō Kaja says he has things to do here at home, and suggests sending Jirō Kaja. The Master says Jirō Kaja is busy, so Tarō Kaja must do as he was told.

Tarō Kaja, still to lazy to go, pretends he has gotten a cramp in his leg suddenly. The Master puts dust on his forehead (a supposed cure for cramps). Tarō Kaja says that this is no ordinary cramp, but one he inherited from his parents. The Master thinks this a strange thing to inherit, and Tarō Kaja explains that he was the youngest of many sons, and when his parents died they distributed their possessions, but by the time they got to him, there was nothing left but this cramp, so that's what he received.

The Master, of course, knows he is lying, so he says that his uncle invited him to bring Tarō Kaja and come to dinner this evening, but since Tarō Kaja is thus incapacitated, he promised to go, but sent word that Tarō Kaja would not be able to.

Tarō Kaja explains that he can command his cramp to go

242

away in cases like this. The Master orders him to get rid of it quick. Tarō Kaja talks to his cramp, and it goes away. The Master orders him to walk here and there, run and jump, then says that the story about the uncle was a lie, and that Tarō Kaja must go get the provisions as he was told.

The cramp comes back again suddenly, and the Master chases Tarō Kaja off scolding.

SHIDŌHŌGAKU　止動方角
(Shidōhōgaku, the Horse)　和大

Shite	TARŌ KAJA
Ado	MASTER
Koado	UNCLE (OF MASTER)
3rd Ado	HORSE

The Master orders Tarō Kaja to go borrow a box of tea, a

sword, and a horse from his Uncle because he has a tea ceremony meeting to attend. Tarō Kaja objects that one person
cannot possible bring all those things at one time, but since
the Master has no other servants, he insists that Tarō Kaja go
alone.

The Uncle willingly lends all the things the Master ordered,
but reminds Tarō Kaja to make sure these things are returned
after the Master is finished with them, because he has never
returned anything he has borrowed before. Tarō Kaja assures him that he himself will make sure everything is returned.
The Uncle also tells him that the Horse has a bad habit of rear-
ing whenever someone coughs behind it, and teaches Tarō
Kaja the magic words necessary to quiet the Horse, which
includes the Horse's name, Shidōhōgaku.

The Master gets impatient, and goes out to look for Tarō
Kaja, and they meet on the road. The Master, in a rage, shoves
Tarō Kaja off the Horse, and jumps on himself, then changes
his mind, and says to walk behind, then ahead again, once more
behind, all the while complaining about everything.

Tarō Kaja gets fed up with the whole affair, goes behind the
Horse and coughs. The Horse immediately rears, and throws
the Master. Tarō Kaja immediately calms the Horse with the
magic words.

The Master somewhat humbled by the fall refuses to ride
the Horse, orders Tarō Kaja to ride it, and takes the sword and
tea box, and begins carrying them himself.

Tarō Kaja feels so important riding the Horse that he says
he would like to know what it feels like to be a Master. The
Master says that since they have changed positions, they might
as well changes roles for a while, since there is no one else in
the area.

Tarō Kaja is shy at first, but soon gets the feel of his assumed

244

role, and repeats word for word and insult for insult the tirade his Master had just before poured out at him. This makes the Master even angrier than before, so he kicks Tarō Kaja off the Horse, and jumps on its back once more. Tarō Kaja, surprised and angry, goes behind the Horse and coughs. The Horse throws the Master and runs away. Tarō Kaja begins to repeat the magic words over the fallen Master who gets up and chases Tarō Kaja off.

SHIMIZU 清水 I O
(A Demon for Better Working Conditions) 和大

| Shite | TARŌ KAJA |
| Ado | MASTER |

The Master calls Tarō Kaja, and orders him to go to Shimizu to draw water for tea. Tarō Kaja says he is busy, but the Master insists. He gives Tarō Kaja a special pail which he values very highly, instructs him not to lose it, and sends him after the water.

Tarō Kaja, who thinks himself above this sort of errand, decides to put a stop to this sort of order. He puts the pail down, and runs screaming back to his Master's house. The Master asks what the matter is, and where his precious pail is. Tarō Kaja answers that he had been chased by a demon, and was so frightened that he threw the pail in the demon's face, after which he heard a crunching sound. The Master orders him to go look for the pail but he refuses, and the Master goes out to find it himself.

Tarō Kaja puts on a mask and dresses up like a demon, runs out ahead of the Master, frightens the Master to death, and makes him promise to give Tarō Kaja plenty of *saké* to drink, to give him a mosquito net to sleep under in the summer, and to pay his back wages. In return for these promises, the "demon" lets the Master go.

When the Master reaches home, Tarō Kaja is there waiting for him. The Master begins to tell Tarō Kaja about how the demon was concerned about Tarō Kaja's welfare. He suddenly realizes that the voice of the demon and Tarō Kaja are the same, and that he has been duped.

The Master says he is going out again to look for his precious pail. When the "demon" appears again, he snatches off the mask under which he finds Tarō Kaja, who he chases off.

In the Ōkura script, the Demon doesn't mention Tarō Kaja's back wages. Tarō Kaja goes out to meet his Master instead of waiting at home. The rest is the same as the Izumi script.

SHINBAI 真奪 　　　　　　　　　　I O
(The Pine Branch and the Sword) 　　和 大

Shite	TARŌ KAJA
Ado	MASTER
Koado	PASSER-BY

The Master takes Tarō Kaja along to look for a subject branch (the main branch for a flower arrangement). On the way they meet a Passer-by who has a beautiful pine branch. They ask him for it, but he says he has promised it to a friend. The Master orders Tarō Kaja to take it by force. Tarō Kaja and the Passer-by stuggle, during which Tarō Kaja gets the branch, and the Passer-by gets the sword Tarō Kaja was carrying, and runs off happily.

Tarō Kaja triumphantly presents the branch to his Master. The Master asks what happened to the sword, and Tarō Kaja realizes it is gone.

They wait for the Passer-by to come back on his way home. The Master grabs him, and orders Tarō Kaja to get something to tie him up with. Tarō Kaja finds a rope which is half twisted, and proceeds to twist it. The Master shouts at him to hurry. The Passer-by struggles to get free knocking Tarō Kaja over several times in the process. Finally Tarō Kaja gets ready, but in the confusion, ties up the Master instead of the Passer-by. The Passer-by runs off happily, still in possession of the sword. The Master and Tarō Kaja get to their feet and chase off after the Passer-by.

SHUJŌ 柱杖 (The New Staff) I 和

Shite	PRIEST
Ado	STAFF MAKER
Koado	WIFE (OF STAFF MAKER)

A Priest goes to pick up a new staff he had ordered some time before. The Staff Maker asks about the life of a priest, and asks the Priest to shave his head and let him become an acolyte. The Priest questions him to make sure he knows what he is doing, and whether he has permission from his family, and especially from his Wife. The Staff Maker assures him he has considered it for quite some time, and that everyone is in favor of it.

The Priest then agrees to perform the rites. The Staff Maker's Wife comes in just as the Priest finishes shaving the Staff

Maker's head, and she flies into a rage when she sees what is happening. She grabs the razor and chases the Priest off. Next she flies at her husband, who says the Priest forced him to do it. She chases him off scolding.

SHŪKUGARAKASA　秀句傘
(The Riddle Umbrella)

I O
和 大

Shite	DAIMYŌ
Ado	TARŌ KAJA
Koado	UMBRELLA MAKER

A Daimyō calls Tarō Kaja and asks him what it is that people are always laughing about at various gatherings. Tarō Kaja says that it is a kind of double entendre riddle called *shūku*. The Daimyō asks if one can learn to make these riddles. Tarō Kaja says yes, and the Daimyō asks to be taught. Tarō Kaja says that he is not good enough at it to teach, so the Daimyō sends him out to find someone who can teach *shūku*. Tarō Kaja meets an Umbrella Maker on the road, and the Umbrella Maker says he can make any number of *shūku* about umbrellas. They return and the Daimyō is so pleased with his teacher that he gives him his sword, dagger, fan, and the clothes off his back. In return the Umbrella Maker gives the Daimyō his last umbrella, and goes off singing happily.

In the Ōkura script, the Umbrella Maker leaves quietly as soon as he gives the Daimyō the umbrella. The Daimyō recites a poem about cold rain at night and an umbrella, then observes that *shūku* is a rather chilly pastime.

248

SHŪRON 宗論 (A Religious Dispute)   I   O
和   大

> Shite   NEMBUTSU PRIEST (JŌDO)
> Ado   HOKKE PRIEST
> Koado   INNKEEPER

Two Priests meet on the road to the capital, and decide to travel together, but when they discover they are of different sects, the Nembutsu Priest decides to tease the Hokke Priest who wants nothing better than to be left alone, and to get away from the Nembutsu Priest as quickly as possible.

The Nembutsu Priest teases the Hokke Priest by blessing him with his rosary, and the Hokke Priest does the same in return, but not in fun. He tries to get away by sneaking into a house by the road, and asking for lodging, but the Nembutsu Priest finds him, and requests lodging in the same house.

They try to convert each other, but the Hokke Priest soon gets bored and goes to sleep. The next morning, they try to out pray each other with their morning prayers, till the noise reaches such a point that they get confused and begin saying each other's prayers. When they realize what has happened, they are both embarrassed, become friends, and go off singing and dancing together.

SŌHACHI 宗八 (A Priest and a Cook)   I   O
(Ōkura title written: 惣八)
和   大

> Shite   COOK
> Ado   WEALTHY MASTER
> Koado   PRIEST

A Wealthy Master puts up a sign advertising that he wants to hire a priest and a cook. A Priest comes along who has been a cook till recently, but got tired of cooking and became a priest because it seemed like a simpler life. Next a Cook named Sōhachi, who has till recently been a priest, but since he became bored with the tedious work of a priest became a cook, arrives on the scene.

The Master hires these two, puts them to work, and goes out on business (in the Ōkura script he just goes to another room). The two confess to each other, and each begins teaching the other his new trade. The Master returns, and gets angry when he finds them doing each other's work. They get confused, pick up the wrong tools and begin to work. The Master scolds them and chases them off.

SORA UDE 空腕 (The Brave Coward)　　I　O
和　大

Shite　　TARŌ KAJA
Ado　　　MASTER

Tarō Kaja, who is actually a terrible coward, has a bad habit of bragging about his bravery and prowess. His Master decides to cure him of this habit, so he sends Tarō Kaja out to get some fish about dusk. Since he must pass along a rather long lonely road, he asks to borrow his Master's sword.

Just as he reaches the loneliest part of the road, he is frightened first by a thicket, and then simply by shadows which he imagines to be a group of evil men, and offers the sword in return for his life. The Master, in the meantime, has gotten worried about him, and going out to look for him, finds him grovelling in the dust offering up the sword as ransom. The Master grabs the sword and taps Tarō Kaja on the back, at which, thinking he has been sliced in two, he falls into a dead faint. The Master goes home to wait for his return.

When Tarō Kaja comes to, he at first thinks he has died and is in heaven, but soon recognizes his surroundings, discovers he is not even wounded, and takes off for home as fast as he can run.

The Master asks for the sword and Tarō Kaja proceeds to tell a long gory story of the terrific fight he had with dozens of *samurai* in which he fought so hard and killed so many that the sword broke in two and he threw it away.

The Master shows Tarō Kaja the sword, and he marvels that it is in one piece again, saying that it must be a miraculous sign of good luck. The Master tells him what really happened, and scolds him soundly.

SUEHIRO 末広
(An Umbrella instead of a Fan)

一〇
和大

Shite   MASTER
Ado   TARŌ KAJA
Koado   SELLER OF UMBRELLAS

The Master sends his servant Tarō Kaja to the capital to buy a *suehirogari*. *Suehirogari* is just another word for fan, but Tarō Kaja does not know this. He reaches the capital and realizes that he has come without asking for a description of the thing he is supposed to buy, so he begins shouting that he wants to buy a *suehirogari*.

A dishonest Umbrella Seller realizes Tarō Kaja's lack of

knowledge, and sells him an old umbrella. The Master has ordered a *suehirogari* with good strong paper, polished bones, and pictures painted on it. (*zare-e* meaning "pictures" can also means a handle to strike with.) The Umbrella Seller explains that this umbrella has all these things, and demands an exorbitant price. As a special service, the Umbrella Seller also teaches Tarō Kaja a song to make his Master feel good when he becomes unhappy. Tarō Kaja returns home, and is, of course, scolded for his mistake, and is chased out of the house. He begins singing and dancing the song he was taught, the Master hears him, comes out to watch and finally begins dancing with him. After the song and dance, he rewards Tarō Kaja for his cleverness.

SUEHIROGARI 末広がり (*See* Suehiro)

SUGOROKU 双六 (Backgammon)

I
和

Shite	GHOST OF KUROZŌ
Ado	PRIEST
Koado	TWO ACCOMPANYING PRIESTS
Koado	VILLAGER

A Priest and his two companion Priests are very fond of Backgammon, so they are on their way to visit a very famous Backgammon player named Kurozō. As they near the area where Kurozō is supposed to be living, they come across a grave. They ask a Villager whose grave it is, and he explains it is the grave of Kurozō who died playing Backgammon. The Priests pray for Kurozō's soul.

Kurozō's Ghost appears, thanks them for their prayers, and tells them the story of his life and death, and of his love for Backgammon. Then he returns to his grave to rest in peace.

This one of the Nōgakari Kyōgen, meaning it is composed on the Noh structure.

SU HAJIKAMI 酢薑
(Vinegar and Ginger)

I   O
和   大

Shite	VINEGAR SELLER
Ado	GINGER SELLER

A Vinegar Seller from Izumi and a Ginger Seller from Tsu meet in the capital, and quarrel over the right to sell their wares in the area. They both try to prove their inherited rights in chanted narratives (katari) in which they use the name of their

wares in double entendre. They both have impressive family trees, so they decide to compete with *shūku* (double ententre riddles and repartee) as they walk along. They both like *shūku*, and are so good at it that they completely forget their quarrel in pleasant chatter, and become good friends. They decide to become a team and sell together.

Suddenly they notice that the sun has gone down, make a poem about their new friendship, have one last laugh, and part till the morrow.

SUMINURI 墨塗 I O
(Black Crocodile Tears) 和 大

	Shite	DAIMYŌ
	Ado	TARŌ KAJA
	Koado	WOMAN (DAIMYŌ'S MISTRESS)

A Daimyō, who has finished his business in the capital, calls Tarō Kaja to inform him that they will leave for home soon. Before leaving he must visit his Mistress to tell her good-bye. They go to her house, and she expresses great sorrow at the news. Tarō Kaja notices that her sorrow is being expressed by the use of water from a bowl to simulate tears. He informs the Daimyō of this, but he refuses to believe him, so Tarō Kaja secretly changes the bowl she is using for one full of black ink. The Mistress continues to "cry" and soon her face becomes quite black. The surprised Daimyō confers with Tarō Kaja, and they decide to give the Girl a mirror as a going-away present. She looks in the mirror, gets very angry, and paints the Daimyō's face with the ink. (There are two possible endings to this Kyōgen. In the other, she simply chases him off.)

In the Ōkura script, when the Woman gets angry, the Master says it was Tarō Kaja's doing, at which the Woman smears Tarō Kaja's face with the ink. The rest is the same as the Izumi script.

SUŌ OTOSHI 素袍落   I O
(The Dropped Gift)   和 大

Shite	TARŌ KAJA
Ado	MASTER
Koado	UNCLE

The Master calls Tarō Kaja, and orders him to go tell his Uncle that he is going on a pilgrimage, and is planning to leave the same day. He had promised the Uncle some time back that they would go together. The Master also orders Tarō Kaja not to tell the Uncle that he is going to accompany his Master on the trip.

The Uncle, of course, refuses to go because of the short notice. He asks Tarō Kaja if he is going, Tarō Kaja says, yes, probably since there is no one else his Master can take along, so the Uncle insists on giving him a drink for good luck.

The more Tarō Kaja drinks, the more he criticizes his Master's greed and stinginess, saying that the reason he didn't want the Uncle to know Tarō Kaja was going along was because if the Uncle knew he would treat Tarō Kaja to drinks and gifts in return for which they would be obliged to bring back souveniers for the Uncle, all his family and his servants. Tarō Kaja praises the Uncle for his generosity and kindness, drinks more and more, gets drunker and drunker, begins repeating himself and getting things all mixed up.

Finally Tarō Kaja says he must be on his way, and the Uncle gives him a ceremonial costume to wear at the shrine, and warns him to hide it from his Master because if the Master sees it, he will surely take it away from him.

Tarō Kaja hides the gift in the breast of his kimono, and staggers toward home singing and dancing merrily.

In the meantime, the Master has become impatient, goes out to look for Tarō Kaja, and finds him staggering along drunk.

Unknown to Tarō Kaja, his gift slips out and falls to the ground, and the Master picks it up quickly and hides it behind his own back. Tarō Kaja discovers his loss and begins searching for it. The Master shows him that he has it, and runs off, with Tarō Kaja close at his heels demanding it back.

In the Ōkura script, the plan is to leave on the trip the next day. At the end, the Master teases Tarō Kaja by showing him the gift after he picks it up. Tarō Kaja grabs it and runs off happily. The Master chases out after him scolding. The rest is the same as the Izumi script.

SUZUKIBŌCHŌ 鱸包丁
(How to Cut Sea-Perch)

Shite   UNCLE
Ado   NEPHEW

The Uncle has just been promoted in rank and has asked his Nephew to bring him a carp in celebration. The Nephew hasn't even made any attempt to get a carp, but goes to his Uncle's house, and tells his Uncle that he caught a very large carp, and tied it in the river to keep it alive, but when he went to get it to bring it, it had been half eaten by something or other, so he threw the rest of it away, and has come to apologize.

The Uncle knows that his Nephew is an incurable liar, and that this story is more than likely one of his tall stories. He decides to teach the Nephew a lesson. He invites the Nephew to stay for a dinner of sea-perch and says that while they are

waiting for it to be prepared, he will tell him how sea-perch is prepared. He goes into great detail about the cutting and preparing, then proceeds to describe all the other delicious things they will eat, then the *saké* they will drink, plus the proper rules for drinking, after which he describes the tea they will drink, and teaches the Nephew the proper etiquette for the tea ceremony. Then he teaches him the proper way to thank his host and say good-bye, which he orders the Nephew to use immediately and go home, because this entertainment is just like his carp, that is, it was eaten by something or other.

The Nephew suddenly realizes he has been found out and royally scolded. He humbly apologizes, and goes quietly on his way.

TACHIBAI 太刀奪 (*See* Tachi Ubai)

TACHI UBAI 太刀奪 (Sword Stealing)   I   O
                                        和 大

Shite	TARŌ KAJA
Ado	MASTER
Koado	PASSER-BY

The Master and Tarō Kaja are on their way to a temple when they see a Passer-by who has a very nice long-sword. The Master admires the sword and since he only has a short-sword, Tarō Kaja offers to steal the long-sword. He borrows his Master's short-sword, and confronts the Passer-by demanding the long-sword. The Passer-by not only refuses, but takes the short-sword as well and goes off happily.

The Master and Tarō Kaja decide to wait in ambush for the

Passer-by to come back this way. When he comes back, they jump him. The Master grabs the Passer-by, and orders Tarō Kaja to get something to tie him up with. In the confusion, Tarō Kaja ties the Master up, and the Passer-by gets away still in possession of both swords. When they realize what has happened, the Master and Tarō Kaja rush off after the Passer-by shouting, "Thief! Help! Thief!"

TAIKO OI 太鼓負 (The Drum Bearer)

I
和

Shite	VILLAGER
Ado	WIFE
Tachishū	WORSHIPPERS

People involved in the Festival:

MASTER OF CEREMONIES

TWO DANCERS

259

TWO PRIESTS
DRUMMER
CHILD
TWO ACOLYTES

It is time for the annual festival, and a certain Villager has been given the part of policeman, which is the same work he has done for many years past. He is a rather shy quiet person, so even though new people have come into the village, and gotten better parts, he has never had the courage to demand a better part for himself. His Wife insists that he demand a better part this time, and sends him off to the mayor's house saying that if he can't get a better part for himself, he need not come home for she won't let him in the house.

He still hasn't come home by the time the parade begins. The Wife regrets her harsh words, and goes out to see what has happened to him.

The Worshippers go to the market, admire the various wares, then take their places to watch the parade.

The parade begins and the Villager appears staggering under the weight of a huge drum. Each of the participants appears and performs his part, all accompanied by the beating of the drum. The Wife, now proud of her husband, tells him he may come back home now. He follows her off, exhausted, but happy.

TAISHI NO TEBOKO　太子手鉾
(The Crown Prince's Halberd)

I
和

Shite　TARŌ KAJA
Ado　　MASTER

260

Tarō Kaja took several days off work without permission, and went on a trip. The Master heard that he has come back home, and goes to his house in a rage. Tarō Kaja explains that he has been home for a few days, but that there has been so much rain, and his roof is in such poor condition, that he has had to stay home to repair the roof and keep his family dry. The Master forgives him, and asks to see the Crown Prince's Halberd which he had heard Tarō Kaja has. At first Tarō Kaja doesn't know what he is talking about, but finally realizes that what the Master has heard about is a tool he has made with a spear and a bamboo stick to mend the roof, and has nicknamed the Crown Prince's Halberd.

Taro Kaja decides to have some fun. He shows this tool to the Master and tries to convince him with a song and dance that this is the very halberd used by Crown Prince Shōtoku. The Master is not impressed, and scolds Tarō Kaja for making fun of him.

TAKARA NO KASA 實の笠   I
(The Magic Straw Hat)   和

Shite	TARŌ KAJA
Ado	MASTER
Koado	SHYSTER

The Master sends Tarō Kaja to the capital to buy some sort of treasure. Tarō Kaja reaches the capital, but not knowing where there is a treasure shop, begins shouting that he wants to buy a treasure. The Shyster offers to help him, and sells him an old straw hat telling him it has the power to make the person who owns it disappear.

261

Tarō Kaja takes the "magic" straw hat home, and when the Master puts it on, he realizes the Shyster had cheated him, because his Master doesn't disappear. Tarō Kaja pretends he can't see the Master. The Master thinks this is great fun, but he wants to see Tarō Kaja disappear. Tarō Kaja explains that only the owner of the hat can use its magic powers. The Master says he will loan Tarō Kaja the hat. Tarō Kaja says it still won't work. The Master says he will give Tarō Kaja the hat. Tarō Kaja refuses with every excuse he can think of, but the Master finally forces him to put it on.

The Master sees that Tarō Kaja doesn't disappear, realizes he has been tricked, and chases Tarō Kaja off scolding him for trying to fool his Master.

TAKARA NO TSUCHI 實の槌 I O
(The Magic Drum Stick) 和 大

Shite   TARŌ KAJA

| Ado | MASTER |
| Koado | SHYSTER (TREASURE SELLER) |

Recently it has become a fad to own a treasure with magic powers, so the Master calls Tarō Kaja, and sends him to the capital to buy such an item.

Tarō Kaja reaches the capital and begins shouting that he wants to buy a treasure with magic powers. A Shyster offers him an old drum stick telling him that if he says certain magic words, and beats the ground, this magic drum stick will produce anything he asks for. Tarō Kaja tries it by asking for a sword, which the Shyster slips under Tarō Kaja's feet, making him think it came from the drum stick.

Tarō Kaja takes it home to his Master, who asks for a black horse. Tarō Kaja tries several times, and since nothing appears, stalls for time by asking for detailed specifications, saying that the Master made noise just as it was about to come out, and finally that it will be wild, so they should wait till some future date, when they can produce it out-of-doors, to which the Master says to let it come out and he will jump on its back and tame it.

In his excitement he mistakes Tarō Kaja for the horse, and jumps on his back. Tarō Kaja soothes the Master's excitement by telling him that he is so positive the Master will soon come into a fortune and be able to build a new house that he can already hear the hammers of the carpenters and blacksmiths.

TAKE NO KO 筍 (Bamboo Sprouts)　　I　O
　　　　　　　　　　　　　　　　　　　　　和　大

Shite　　GROVE OWNER

Ado FARMER
Koado ARBITER

A Farmer gathers bamboo sprouts from his field which is next to a bamboo grove. The Grove Owner accuses him of stealing the sprouts, but the Farmer says that they were from his own field, to which the Grove Owner replies that the roots have come to the field from his grove, and are therefore part of the grove. The Farmer gets angry and strikes the Grove Owner who is lame in one leg. The Grove Owner begins shouting, "Help! This stupid Farmer is attacking a poor helpless cripple!" The Arbiter appears to settle the argument.

The Farmer seems to be in the right to which the Grove Owner finally gives in, but says that he should receive things that come to his grove from the Farmer's field to which the Arbiter agrees. The Grove Owner is referring to a calf that was borne by the farmer's cow when it was in the Grove Owner's grove. This, of course, starts the argument anew, so the Arbiter says that it must be settled by some sort of contest.

The Farmer suggests a poem reciting contest to which the Grove Owner agrees, but they both compose and recite so well, that the matter is still not settled. A *sumō* match is proposed, but the Grove Owner objects because of his bad leg. The Farmer says if the Grove Owner refuses to fight, he must forfeit. The Grove Owner agrees to *sumō*, but when the match begins, he beats the Farmer with a stick, to which the Farmer objects that sticks are against the rules. The Grove Owner explains that since *sumō* is performed with the arms and the legs, and he has one bad leg, the stick should be allowed in place of his bad leg.

The Arbiter suggests, then, that if the stick is taken from the Grove Owner during the match, the Farmer wins. They all agree and proceed with the match.

The Farmer takes the stick, knocks the Grove Owner down and wins. The Grove Owner cries, "I'll let you have both the calf and the bamboo sprouts, but give me back my leg!" The Farmer refuses and runs off. The Grove Owner, unable to stand without the stick, crawls off after him shouting, "Give me back my leg!"

In the Ōkura script, the Farmer agrees to give back the bamboo sprouts if the Grove Owner will return the calf which was borne by his cow in the Grove Owner's grove. The Grove Owner won't agree to this. The Grove Owner's lame leg is not mentioned until the *sumō* match when he begins beating the Farmer with his stick. The rest is the same as the Izumi script.

TAKO 蛸 (The Octopus)　　　Ｉ　Ｏ
和　大

Shite	OCTOPUS
Waki	TRAVELLING PRIEST
Ai	VILLAGER

This Kyōgen is a Nōgakari, meaning it is written in the same form as a Noh Drama, the difference being that the material it deals with is lighter, and in this case rather amusing.

A Travelling Priest arrives at Shimizu Inlet on his way to the capital, and stops to rest by a grave. An Old Man suddenly appears in front of him, says that he is the Spirit of the Octopus and asks the Priest to pray for his soul, then just as suddenly disappears.

The Priest asks a Villager who passes by about this, and the Villager explains that the previous spring, one of the fishermen of the village caught a huge Octopus. It was so large that the whole village fed on it, but after it had been eaten, its Ghost began appearing every night, so they set up this grave marker and it has become the practice to pray for its soul.

The Priest offers up prayers, and the Spirit of the Octopus appears, this time in its true form, and dances while singing a song. It laments having been chopped up, boiled, dried, and eaten by the people.

TANUKI NO HARA TSUZUMI 狸腹鼓 I O
(The Badger's Belly Drum) 和 大

Shite   NUN (ACTUALLY A FEMALE BADGER)
Ado   HUNTER

A Hunter goes out at dusk to hunt badger. He comes to a lonely field and hides in the brush to wait for one to come along.

A female Badger disguised as a Nun comes out to search for her husband who hasn't been home for several days. She is going along the lonely road, singing to keep herself company, when the Hunter sees her and asks what she is doing away from her temple at this time of night. She says she is on her way home. She notices he is a Hunter and gives him a sermon in chanted narrative (*katari*) about the horrors of hell for those who spend their lives on earth killing living things. The Hunter is properly frightened, and promises never to kill anything again.

They part, and the Nun goes happily on her way, till she hears a dog barking and hides in a thicket.

The Hunter continues to look for badgers, finds the Nun in the thicket, realizes he has been tricked, and prepares to shoot her.

The Badger pleads for her life, saying she has children who

will have no one to take care of them if she dies. The Hunter finally agrees to let her go free on the condition that she will beat her "belly drum" for him.

She promises to do anything he asks if he will only let her go free. While she is performing, he changes his mind again, decides that hunting is more fun, and chases her off with his bow and arrow.

In the Ōkura script, the Badger has only come out, disguised as a Nun, to look for food for her many children. The rest is the same as the Izumi script.

TARU MUKO 樽聟
(The Groom and the Saké Jug)

一
和

Shite	GROOM
Ado	FATHER-IN-LAW
Koado	TARŌ KAJA
3rd Ado	FRIEND OF THE GROOM

A Groom on his way to his Father-in-law's house for his ceremonial first visit drops by a Friend's house to ask to borrow a servant to carry the saké jug he is carrying as a gift for the ceremony. The Friend says he is sorry, but all his servants are out on errands, so he will take the part of the servant himself. They arrive at the Father-in-law's house, and the Father-in-law mistakes the Friend for the Groom, and refuses to admit his mistake, even to the point of chasing the Groom out when he gets too noisy about demanding his rights.

The Father-in-law performs the ceremony with the Friend, and gives him a dagger. The Friend goes out and explains to the Groom what has happened. The Groom is angry, grabs the

sword claiming it is rightfully his, and runs off followed by the
Friend who cries, "Give it back to me. He gave it to me, so
it's mine!"

TAUE 田植 (The Rice Planting Ceremony)　　Ｉ
　　　　　　　　　　　　　　　　　　　　　　　　　　　和

Shite	PRIEST
Ado	GIRL (LEADER OF GROUP)
Tachishū	GROUP OF GIRLS

A Priest and a Group of Girls perform the Spring Rice
Planting Ceremony. The Ceremony consists of a light-hearted
song and dance. The song tells of spring, rice planting, birds,
flowers, and love.

TOBIKOE 飛越 (Jump Across)　　　Ｉ　Ｏ
　　　　　　　　　　　　　　　　　　　和　大

Shite	ACOLYTE
Ado	MAN

A Man asks an Acolyte to accompany him to a Tea Ceremony Gathering, because he is very poor at performing the
Tea Ceremony. The Acolyte agrees to go, and on their way,
he teaches the Man a few things about the Tea Ceremony.
Presently they come to a wide river. The Man jumps across
without any trouble, but the Acolyte cannot get up enough
courage to make the leap. He tries several times, but fails, first
blaming his inability on the Man, because he coughed at the

crucial moment, next on his eyes which he says are cowardly, and then when he closes his eyes and tries to jump, the Man stops him because of the danger of falling in. Finally the Man offers his hand to help him jump across, but this only ends in the Acolyte's falling in the middle of the river and getting thoroughly drenched. The Man laughs at the sight, the Acolyte gets angry, and tells the Man he has seen him in an even funnier position. The Man says that is impossible, whereupon the Acolyte tells of the time when the Man lost a *sumō* match to a man half his size. The Man gets angry at this, and challenges the Acolyte to a match then and there. The Acolyte tries to run away but the Man catches him, throws him down and runs off gleefully. The Acolyte shouts after him that the victor cannot be decided in only one round.

In the Ōkura script, the Man simply promised to take the Acolyte with him the next time he goes to a Tea Ceremony Gathering because the Acolyte is especially fond of the Tea Ceremony. The rest is the same as the Izumi script.

TŌJIN KODAKARA　唐人子宝　　I
(The Chinaman and his Devoted Son)　和

Shite	CHINAMAN
Ado	MASTER
Koado	TARŌ KAJA
Koado	CHINAMAN'S SON

The Master hired a Chinaman as an interpreter, but since he has no interpreting work to be done, he has given the Chinaman the job of cutting grass. No grass has been cut the last few days, so the Master calls Tarō Kaja and asks him what has

269

happened to the Chinaman. Tarō Kaja explains that the Chinaman's Son has come to visit him, and he doesn't want his Son to find out he cuts grass for a living, so he has taken off work.

The Master calls the Chinaman, and asks to meet his Son. The Chinaman brings his Son and explains that his Son has brought gifts for the Master, and that he has promised his mother that he would not return home without his Father. The Master is very impressed with the Son's love for his Father, and gives the Chinaman permission to go home with his Son. The Chinaman is very happy. He describes the gifts his Son has brought in a song, then he and the Master sing a song of parting.

TŌJINZUMŌ 唐人相撲 (Chinese Sumō) I O
和 大

Shite   EMPEROR OF CHINA
Ado   JAPANESE SUMŌ WRESTLER
Koado   INTERPRETER
Tachishū TWO OR FOUR CHINESE CHILDREN
Tachishū SEVERAL CHINAMEN

A Japanese *Sumō* Wrestler, having been in China for a long time, becomes homesick, and decides to return to Japan. He goes to ask permission from the Emperor. The Emperor grants the permission, but orders that he wrestle once more before he leaves. The Wrestler consents, and prepares himself for the match. He beats all the Chinese present, and finally the Emperor decides to wrestle, and is also beaten, and carried off by his retainers.

This Kyōgen is seldom performed because of the number

of performers necessary. The unusual point of interest is that the Chinese all speak in meaningless Chinese-like sounds, and the Interpreter translates this into Japanese.

TOKORO 野老 (The Mountain Potato)　　I
和

Shite	TOKORO (MOUNTAIN POTATO)
Waki	PRIEST
Ai	VILLAGER

This Kyōgen is a Nōgakari, meaning it is composed in the form of a Noh Drama, but with lighter subject matter.

A Priest on his way to the capital sees an unusual grave marker, and asks a passing Villager about it. The Villager explains that the previous year at about the same time, one of the Villagers dug up an exceptionally large Tokoro (Mountain Potato). All the villagers feasted on it, then decided since it was so big that it must have a soul, so they set up this memorial grave marker. The Villager asks the Priest to pray for its soul.

While the Priest is praying, the Spirit of the Tokoro appears, and in a song and dance tells of his pain and suffering, when parts of his body were being prepared for cooking, cooked in various ways, and finally eaten by various people.

TSŪEN 通圓 (Tsūen, the Tea Priest)　　I　O
和　大

Shite	GHOST OF TSŪEN
Waki	PRIEST
Ai	VILLAGER

This Kyōgen is a Nōgakari, meaing it is written in the form of a Noh Drama.

A Priest comes along the road to a tea house, and finds it without a priest in charge of making and serving tea. He asks the reason of a Villager who tells him that this tea house belonged to a Priest named Tsūen. It has been kept as a memorial since he died, and that today is the anniversary of his death. Then the Villager asks the Priest to pray for Tsūen's soul. The Priest begins to pray, and the Ghost of Tsūen appears, tells the story of his life, dances, and serves the Priest tea.

TSUKIMI ZATŌ　月見座頭　　　　　　　　　　　O
(The Moon-Viewing Blind Man)　　　　　　　　　大

Shite　　　BLIND MAN
Ado　　　PASSER-BY

A Blind Man goes out moon-viewing alone on the night of

272

August 15th which is considered the best night of the year for moon-viewing. Since he can't see the moon, he enjoys himself listening to the sounds of various insects.

A Passer-by who has come out moon-viewing sees the Blind Man, and asks him what he is doing. They begin talking, exchange poems, and the Passer-by offers the Blind Man a drink. The more they drink, the more friendly they get. They sing and dance for each other, and finally they go their separate ways, seemingly fast friends and in a happy mood.

The Passer-by decides to tease the Blind Man a little, so he goes back and bumps into him on purpose, they argue, and the Passer-by throws the Blind Man down, and runs off.

The Blind Man sadly searches for his cane, picks himself up, and continues on his way home, musing about how nice the first man was, and how cruel the second was. Not knowing all the while that both the friendly man and the cruel one were the same person.

TSUKUSHI NO OKU 筑紫奥 (Laughs After Taxes)

一〇
和大

Shite	FARMER FROM TANBA
Ado	FARMER FROM TSUKUSHI
Koado	TAX COLLECTOR

A Farmer from Tsukushi bringing cloth, and one from Tanba bringing fruit meet on the way to the capital to pay their annual taxes, and decide to travel together. They reach their destination, and find that they both pay their taxes in the same place. They have both brought such an unusually large amount that the Tax Collector rewards them. The Farmers are so happy that they laugh very loud. The Tax Collector scolds them for being so noisy, and orders them to laugh again, once for each unit of land they farm. The Farmers argue over who should laugh first, and finally they decide to laugh together. On their way out, they decide to go back, and make the Tax Collector laugh too. They go back and tickle the Tax Collector. He insists that they laugh with him, so they all three laugh together.

In the Ōkura script, the Farmers do their laughing separately. There is also a great deal more detail in the dialogue. The rest is the same as the Izumi script.

TSUKUZUKUSHI 土筆 (*See* Uta Arasoi)

TSURIBARI 釣針   I O
(The Capricious Magic Fish Hook)   和 大

Shite   TARŌ KAJA
Ado   MASTER
Koado   MASTER'S NEW WIFE
Tachishū   WOMEN

The Master takes his servant Tarō Kaja and goes to Nishinomiya to pray for a wife. Tarō Kaja is also still single, so they both want new wives. They reach the shrine, pray, and sleep. When the Master wakes up, he has had a dream in which he was informed that he would find a fish hook near the Western Gate, and if he will throw this fish hook into the sea, he will catch a new wife.

They take the fish hook home, and the Master has Tarō

Kaja throw it in the sea near their home. He catches a beautiful Wife for his Master, then several Girls to serve as maids for the new Wife, and finally gets permission to fish for a wife for himself.

The Master, his new Wife, and her Maids all go into the house. Tarō Kaja is very happy to have a Wife. He is very embarrassed, but finally works up enough courage to speak to her. He hasn't seen her face yet because it is covered with a veil. She is reluctant to take off the veil, and finally Tarō Kaja pulls it off himself. She is so ugly that Tarō Kaja can't imagine himself married to her, and tries to run away. She catches hold of him, he gets loose and runs off, the Wife following close behind.

In the Ōkura script, the fish hook is received as a reward for faithful worship, not specifically to use to fish for a wife, but for anything the Daimyō wants. The Daimyō has Tarō Kaja fish for a sword and a dagger, then Tarō Kaja suggests a Wife for the Daimyō, then ladies-in-waiting for the Wife. Tarō Kaja gets permission to choose a wife for himself from among the Ladies-in-waiting. He looks at them all, finds them all ugly, and tries to run away from them, but they say they won't let him go till he chooses a wife. He finally breaks through their line and gets away. They all run out after him.

TSURIGITSUNE 釣狐 (Fox Trapping) 　I O
　　　　　　　　　　　　　　　　　　　　　　　和 大

> Shite　　FOX
> Ado　　　TRAPPER

An Old Fox changes himself into the Trapper's Uncle Hakuzōsu, who is a priest, and goes to the Trapper's house to warn him against trapping foxes. He tells the Trapper a long story about foxes who changed into people and took revenge in various ways. The Trapper promises to stop trapping foxes, and throws away his traps.

On the way home, the Fox finds one of the traps in the middle of the road, set and baited with fried mice. He wants to eat the bait, but decides to go home and change himself back to his original form before he tries to steal it.

In the meantime, the Trapper comes out to look at the trap he had supposedly thrown away, and finds paw prints all around it. He realizes that Hakuzōsu was actually the Old Fox he has been trying to catch. He is sure the Old Fox will return for the bait, so he waits behind a tree.

Sure enough the Fox comes back, tries to get the bait, and gets caught, but before the Trapper can get to him, he gets loose again, and runs away. The Trapper takes off after him yelling, "Somebody help me catch the sly old Fox!"

TSURUSHI 弦師
(The Cowardly Bow String Maker)

I
和

Shite   BOW STRING MAKER
Ado   PASSER-BY

A Bow String Maker runs on crying and trembling. A Passer-by asks him what is wrong. He explains that he went to deliver some bow strings, and stayed longer than he had planned, so that it was dusk when he started on his way home. When he came to Gojō Bridge, he thought he saw a man that must have been Ushiwaka (Yoshitsune) who drew his sword and slashed at him. He imagines that he is dying, but when the Passer-by asks him where it hurts, he realizes he doesn't hurt at all, so he dries his tears. The Passer-by realizes that the Bow String Maker is a terrible coward, and decides to tease him. The Passer-by tells him that his back is split wide open and covered with blood, at which the Bow String Maker again begins to weep and wail. The Passer-by admits it was a joke, and the Bow String Maker once again dries his tears. The Passer-by says it was probably all his imagination, and that he is just a coward. The Bow String Maker gets angry and retorts that if he had seen it, he would be scared too.

The Passer-by gets tired of listening to his whimpering, and says he can see the man with the sword coming this way. The Bow String Maker screams and grabs ahold of the Passer-by for protection. The Passer-by tries to shake him off and get away, but he holds on for dear life.

TSUTO YAMABUSHI 苞山伏   I
(The Lunch Thief)   和

Shite	FOOD THIEF
Ado	MOUNTAINEER
Koado	YAMABUSHI

A Mountaineer lays down by the side of the road to take a nap. A Yamabushi comes by and decides to take a nap close by. A Food Thief happens along, sees them sleeping, steals the Mountaineer's lunch, and is eating it when the Mountaineer begins to stir. The Food Thief throws the lunch wrapper down by the Yamabushi. The Mountaineer wakes up, starts to eat his lunch and finds it missing. He wakes the others up, and·all three accuse each other of having eaten the lunch.

The Yamabushi finally suggests that the only way to solve the problem, since all three of them are the possible thief, is to pray and the prayer will point out the real thief. He prays and the Food Thief is suddenly seized with pain, and collapses unable to move. The Mountaineer wants to kill the culprit on the spot, but the Yamabushi insists that he has suffered enough. The Yamabushi prays while holding the Mountaineer back. The Food Thief finally gets up and staggers off. The Mountaineer tries to catch the Food Thief, and the Yamabushi continues to block his path.

TSUTSU SASAE 筒竹筒   I
(The Saké Container)   和

Shite	GOD OF THE DOVE
Ado	SAKÉ PEDDLER FROM YAMATO
Koado	SAKÉ PEDDLER FROM KŌCHI

Two *Saké* Peddlers, one from Yamato and one from Kōchi meet on the road, and in the course of their conversation, discover that they are both going to the Hachiman Shrine to give thanks for another good year. One calls his bamboo *saké* container *tsutsu* and the other calls his *sasae*. They get into an argument over which is the correct name. In the middle of their quarrel a Stranger appears and identifies himself as the God of the Dove, and says he has been sent from the god Hachiman to find out what they were discussing, and to lead them safely to the temple. He listens to their story and informs them, by telling them a story in chanted narrative (*katari*), that both words are correct, thus there is nothing to quarrel about. He asks them for *saké*, then performs a song and dance for them.

UCHIZATA　内沙汰
(The Trial Rehearsal)
(Ōkura title: Oko Sako　右近左近)

Shite	OKO, THE FARMER
Ado	WIFE

Oko tells his Wife that he is planning to go to the Grand Ise Shrine with some of the neighbors, and asks if she will go along. She says that she would be happy to go, till she hears Sako is going. Suddenly she changes her mind and says that she is too embarrassed to go because everyone else is rich enough to have something to ride on. Oko says that he has a cow she can ride on. She laughs at him and asks him where he got a cow. He explains that one day recently Sako's cow was eating in his field. He caught it and told it that he would claim it at the end of the year, and it answered, "Moo," and that at the same time Sako smiled in consent. She laughs at him and says Sako was only laughing at his stupidity.

Oko gets angry, and says he will take the case to court and see who is right. She continues to make fun of him, saying that he is such a coward that he would never get his case even heard, let alone win, and suggests that before he goes, she will play the part of the judge so he can rehearse what he is going to say.

First they rehearse Sako's plea which Oko performs well, but when it comes time to play himself, he is so frightened that he can't even get the story straight, and the Wife plays the part of the judge so forbiddingly that Oko finally passes out.

When Oko comes to, he accuses his Wife of being on Sako's side. In fact, he relates an story about when he saw his Wife and Sako talking very intimately. The Wife is so angry at being found out that she beats Oko with a stick, knocks him down, and goes off in a huff. Oko picks himself up and yells out after her, "Well anyway, now I know for sure you are Sako's mistress."

In the Ōkura script, Oko begins by telling his Wife that he is going to take Sako to court. The scene where Oko plays the part of Sako is not in the Ōkura script, and the play ends with Oko and his Wife beating and screaming at each other.

UGUISU 鶯 (The Nightingale)

一
和

Shite   NOBLEMAN
Ado   NIGHTINGALE KEEPER

A Nightingale Keeper takes his nightingale out to a field to give it some fresh air and hear it sing. He puts its cage in the middle of the field, and sits down some distance away to listen.

A Nobleman whose lord is very fond of nightingales wants to present one to his lord, but he has no money to buy one. Even though he has no experience, he goes out with a long bamboo pole to hunt. He comes to the field, hears the nightingale singing, finds it in its cage, picks it up, and starts to go off with it when he is stopped by the Nightingale Keeper.

The Nightingale Keeper informs the Nobleman that the bird is his. The Nobleman says, "Then sell it to me. I have no money now, but will pay you next time I see you." The Nightingale Keeper objects that they have never met before, and they are not likely to meet again, and asks for the Nobleman's sword as surety.

The Nobleman then suggests a wager to settle the deal. He says that if he catches the nightingale, it is his, but if he misses it, the Nightingale Keeper will win not only his nightingale, but also the sword. The Nightingale Keeper objects that anyone can catch a bird in a cage, but the Nobleman explains that he has absolutely no experience. The Keeper agrees, but on the condition that the Nobleman can have only one try.

The Nobleman tries and misses. He wants another chance, so this time he bets his dagger. He misses again, thus losing his sword, his dagger, and the nightingale. He tells a story about his lord in a chanted narrative (*katari*), then goes off singing sadly about his losses.

UOZEKKYŌ 魚説経 (*See* Uozeppō)

UOZEPPŌ 魚説法 (The Fish Sermon)　　I　O
(Ōkura title: Uozekkyō 魚説経　　　　　　　和　大

Shite　　ACOLYTE (ŌKURA: FISHERMAN)

A Wealthy Man goes to a temple to request the head priest to come and perform the dedication service for a new memorial he has built for his dead father. The head priest is not in, so the Man finally convinces the Acolyte to go with him. The Acolyte doesn't know how to perform a proper service, so since he lived in a fishing village during his boyhood, he decides to use the names of fish in double entendre to make something that sounds like a sermon. The Man realizes what the Acolyte is doing, scolds him for using such smelly words in the dedication, and chases him off. The Acolyte continues to use the names of fish in his protests at being roughly treated.

In the Ōkura script, a Fisherman from Tsu who is down on his luck has decided to try his luck as a priest. The Wealthy Man comes out to the highway to look for a priest to perform the dedication ceremony, and hires the Fisherman. At the end, the Wealthy Man discovers the truth, the Fisherman apologizes, and the Wealthy Man chases him off scolding. The rest is the same as the Izumi script.

URI NUSUBITO   瓜盗人   I O
(The Melon Thief)   和 大

Shite   THIEF
Ado   FARMER

The Farmer comes out to tend his melon patch, sees the melons are nearly ripe, and puts up a fence and a scarecrow to scare away birds and beasts.

A Man down on his luck, who is not really a thief at all,

decides to try his hand at stealing melons. He breaks through the fence and begins looking for melons. It is night and he has trouble finding any. He has heard that the way to find melons at night is to roll around in the patch. He rolls around, finds several nice melons, and finally runs into the scarecrow. Thinking it is a real person, he begs for his life explaining he is not a real thief, but just a man down on his luck who has come to borrow a few melons. When the scarecrow doesn't move or answer, the Thief realizes his mistake. In anger at being tricked, he knocks the scarecrow down, pulls up the melon vines, and leaves with several melons.

The Farmer comes back the next morning, and finds that he has been robbed. Since a thief always returns to the scene of his crime, the Farmer dresses himself up as the scarecrow and waits. The Thief sure enough comes back for more melons, sees the scarecrow, but this time is not only not frightened, but since it is so well made decides to use it as his partner, and get in a little practice of the song and dance, which depicts a demon and a sinner in hell, which he will perform on a float in the coming festival. While he is thus playing with the scarecrow, he discovers his mistake, and takes off at a dead run with the Farmer close at his heels.

In the Ōkura script, the Thief had stolen melons from the same patch the night before, given them to someone who liked them so well that they asked for more, so he has come back to fill the order. He jumps over the fence. Thus the night when the Farmer poses as the scarecrow is the third time the Thief comes. The rest is the same as the Izumi script.

URUSASHI　右流左止
(Mind Your Own Business!)

I
和

Shite	TŌZŌ SHIOAKI
Ado	TEA SHOP GIRL

Tōzō, an old man who is quite a patron of the arts, has retired, and is travelling around the country sightseeing. He comes to Akashi Bay, and decides to rest at a tea shop and enjoy the view.

Tōzō asks the Tea Shop Girl various things about the surrounding area, and finally begins asking her personal questions. She tells him to mind his own business (*urusai*), and he proceeds to tell her a long chanted narrative (*katari*) about the origin of the word. After he is finished, she recites some poems in which the word is used. He is surprised at her knowledge and asks her to become his teacher after he has seen the capital. She agrees and they sing a parting song promising to meet again soon.

USHI NUSUBITO　牛盗人 (The Cow Thief)

I
和

Shite	HYŌGO SABURŌ
Ado	COW KEEPER
Koado	TARŌ KAJA
Koado	JIRŌ KAJA
Koado	CHILD

The Cow Keeper for the Emperor discovers that one of the Emperor's cows has been stolen. He puts up a sign declaring whoever will give information as to the identity or the whereabouts of the Thief will be forgiven any crime, or given anything he asks for.

Before long a Child appears, saying that he wishes to report the name and the whereabouts of the thief. He says the thief is Hyōgo Saburō who lives in the next village.

The Cow Keeper sends Tarō Kaja and Jirō Kaja to go arrest the culprit. They soon drag him in, and before long he confesses his crime. He also reveals to them the fact that the Child is his son. He curses and disowns his Child for being a traitor.

They ask him why he stole the cow, and he says it was to pay for a memorial service for his father, and goes on to recite a passage from Buddhist scripture which would seem to sanction such an action. The Cow Keeper says that no matter, the crime is still the same according to law, and Hyōgo Saburō must be put to death.

At this point the Child speaks up demanding his reward. They ask him what he wants, and he answers, "The life of Hyōgo Saburō spared." He goes on to explain that when he saw the sign, he decided that this was the only way to save his Father's life. Father and Son burst into tears. The Father pleads for forgiveness from his Son for his harsh words of a few minutes before. The Cow Keeper and his servants are moved by this display of the Child's love for his Father. They grant him full pardon, and Father and Son set out for home singing for joy.

UTA ARASOI 歌争 (The Poem Fight) I O
(Ōkura title: Tsukuzukushi 土筆)

		和 大

Shite   MAN I
Ado   MAN II

Man II goes to Man I's house to invite him on an outing.
Man I accepts the invitation, but first shows Man II his new
garden. Man II admires the garden and recites a poem about it.
Man I laughs at him for a mistake he made. They go out, and
during their walk, they see some flowers. Man I recites a poem
about the flowers, and Man II laughs at his mistakes at which
Man I gets angry, and says that he can remember something
very amusing about Man II. Man II says it couldn't be nearly
as hilarious as Man I's mistake, so Man I proceeds to tell the
story of when Man II was defeated in *sumō* by a very little man.
Man II gets angry and challenges Man I to a *sumō* match. Man
I tries to run away, but Man II finally catches him, throws him,
and runs off claiming he has won. Man I shouts that the victor
cannot be decided after only one round.

In the Ōkura script, Man I goes to Man II's house, and they
go out together. Man I recites both poems, makes mistakes in
both, and Man II laughs at him both times. Man I gets angry,
and challenges Man II to a *sumō* match. The rest is the same as
the Izumi script.

UTSUBOZARU 靱猿   I   O
(The Monkey Skin Quiver)   和 大

Shite	DAIMYŌ
Ado	TARŌ KAJA
Koado	MONKEY TRAINER
Kokata	MONKEY

A Daimyō goes out hunting with his servant Tarō Kaja, and
on the way they meet a Monkey Trainer. The Daimyō wants
to borrow the Monkey's skin to cover his quiver. The Trainer,

287

of course, refuses so the Daimyō gets angry and threatens to kill both the Trainer and the Monkey. The Trainer finally agrees, and asks for a few minutes to say good-bye. He also says that instead of shooting the Monkey with an arrow, which would harm the skin, he will kill it himself. He starts to strike the Monkey, and the Monkey mistakes his action for a signal to perform, so it grabs the stick and uses it as an oar. The Trainer begins to cry, the Daimyō asks the reason, and the Trainer replies that he has raised and trained the Monkey from the time it was born, so it is like a son to him. The Daimyō is greatly moved, and decides not to kill either the Monkey or the Trainer. In gratitude, the Monkey performs, and the Trainer sings. The Daimyō presents his fan, sword, and even his own clothes to the Monkey Trainer, then he begins to dance and perform with the Monkey, thus ending on a happy note.

WAKAME 若和布
(A Girl Poses as Seaweed)

若
和
Ⅰ

Shite	ACOLYTE
Ado	HEAD PRIEST
Koado	SHYSTER
3rd Ado	WOMAN

The Head Priest is happy because he has just built a new temple with the help of the people in the area. He wants to give a banquet to thank the people for their help, so he tells the Acolyte to go to the city to buy some *wakame* (a kind of seaweed). The Acolyte says he doesn't know what *wakame* looks like, but the Head Priest says that it doesn't matter, because if he just asks around, he will be able to find it easy enough. The

Head Priest says to make sure that it is Ise *wakame*, that it must be new, because when it gets old, the color gets bad, and that it should be good and salty.

The Acolyte goes to the city, and begins shouting that he wants to buy some *wakame*. A Shyster hears him, and decides to trick him out of his money.

The Shyster explains his idea to a Woman he has working in his house. They decide to sell her as *wakame* (which also means young woman) to the Acolyte. However she insists that the Shyster come to the country as soon as possible to bring her back home.

The Shyster shows the Woman to the Acolyte saying that this is a *wakame*. The Acolyte thinks this strange because the Head Priest had said it was something to eat while drinking *saké*. The Shyster answers that things that go with *saké* are not always things to eat. And that if one has this *wakame* pour *saké*, the *saké* drinking becomes more pleasant. The Acolyte says it must be from Ise, and the Shyster answers that this Woman was born in Ise. As for the age, this Woman is young and has good color, and when she cries, salt flows from her eyes. The Acolyte buys her and takes her home with him.

When the Head Priest sees what has happened, he, of course, gets very angry, and the more the Acolyte tries to explain, the more the Head Priest gets angry till he can't take any more and throws them both out.

The Acolyte tells the Woman to go back to the city. She asks what he will do, and he answers that there is nothing for him to do but go back and apologize. She invites him to give up the priesthood and become her husband. He objects at first, but she finally convinces him. They get some *saké* and begin to celebrate their marriage in front of the temple, drinking, singing, and dancing.

The Head Priest hears the noise, finds them enjoying themselves, accuses them of defiling the temple, and chases them out.

WAKANA 若菜
(Spring, Girls, and Saké)

I
和

Shite TEA PRIEST (KAIAMI)
Ado DAIMYŌ
Tachishū GIRLS FROM OHARA

It is Spring, and a Daimyō decides to go on an outing to hunt birds, view the flowers, and generally enjoy the scenery. He calls Kaiami, the Priest, and orders him to make preparations to go out. They talk pleasantly as they go along, and finally come to a field of plum trees which are in blossom. They stop to relax under the trees, try to catch a nightingale, and are distracted by a group of lovely girls coming toward them from across the field, carrying bundles of flowers and sticks on their heads and singing a lovely song.

The Daimyō has Kaiami invite them to share a cup of *saké*. They are very shy at first, but Kaiami is most insistent, and they finally consent. Kaiami offers them *saké*, and as soon as they have had a drink, the Leader of the Girls offers to pour *saké* for the Daimyō. This makes the Daimyō very happy, and he orders Kaiami to sing, then to dance.

With this the ice is broken, and they all join in drinking, singing, and dancing one after the other. Finally the Daimyō orders Kaiami to dance again. The song, which the girls sing for Kaiami to dance to this time, indicates in the lyrics that it is getting late and they must be on their way. All are somewhat reluctant to part after such a pleasant afternoon together. They all sing their appreciation to each other as they go their separate ways. This is probably the most lyrically musical of all Kyōgen.

YAO 八尾　(A Sinner With References)

Ⅰ　O
和　大

Shite　　EMMA, THE KING OF HELL
Ado　　SINNER

Emma, the King of Hell, has come upon hard days as a result of all the religions which help sinners get to heaven. Things have gotten so bad that he himself has finally come out to the Crossing of the Six Roads to catch sinners and chase them to Hell.

A Sinner from the country of Yao appears and when Emma tries to catch him, he produces a letter from the Jizō (patron saint) of Yao. The Jizō of Yao had at some time done Emma a favor, and Emma grumbles that he has been taken advantage of ever since by these endless reference letters.

Just as Emma expected, this letter is another request to guide another sinner to Heaven to which he reluctantly complies, and goes on his way grumbling about one more sinner lost to Heaven.

YAKUSUI 薬水　(Medicinal Water)

Ⅰ
和

Shite　　OLD MAN I
Ado　　OLD MAN II
Tachishū　MANY OLD MEN

An Old Man announces to his Friends that a spring of Medicinal Water has just been discovered in the mountains. They all go to drink of the water without telling the old women, saying that when they become young and handsome again they will find beautiful young girls.

They reach the spring which is at the foot of a waterfall, and sing while they drink. As the water begins to take effect, their beards turn from white to black. They jokingly warn each other to be careful not to drink too much, or they will all get so young they will be babies again.

YASE MATSU 瘦松 (Skinny Pine)　　　 I O
(Ōkura title: Kintōzaemon 金藤左衛門　　和 大

　　　Shite　　　MOUNTAIN ROBBER
　　　Ado　　　WOMAN

A Mountain Robber, who is down on his luck, comes to a valley called Skinny Pine to see if he can find someone to rob. When Mountain Robbers have good luck, they say they found a Fat Pine, and when they have bad luck, a Skinny Pine. Since this particular valley is very lonely and they seldom have good luck here, the valley itself has been given the name Skinny Pine.

A Woman comes along, on her way to visit her parents, with a bag full of her personal belongings. The Robber jumps out at her and she drops the bag and runs. While the Robber is examining the contents of the bag, the Woman sneaks back, grabs the Robber's long spear, and threatens him with his life. She forces him to give her not only her own things, but his sword and clothes as well.

In a last attempt at a show of bravery, the Robber grabs the end of the long spear as the Woman starts to leave with her loot, but she is too fast for him. He chases off after her shouting, "Stop that Woman! She has robbed me of everything!"

In the Ōkura script, the Robber introduces himself as Kintōzaemon, and goes to the mountain. He does not give the name of the valley or mention Skinny Pine and Fat Pine. The rest of the story is the same as *Yase Matsu* except that the dialogue is much more detailed, thus making performance time almost double.

YAWATA NO MAE 八幡前   I O
(Groom with Prompter)   和 大

Shite	GROOM
Ado	MAN FROM YAWATA SANGE
Koado	TARŌ KAJA
3rd Ado	FRIEND (OF GROOM)

A Man from Yawata Sange has a beautiful daughter for whom he wishes to find a suitable groom, so he puts up a sign to that effect specifying that only those with some talent need apply. A prospective Groom sees the sign, and wishing to apply takes down the sign. He has no special talent, but he has a good Friend who, he is confident, will be able to teach him something that will qualify him. He confides in the Friend, and they finally decide he will pose as an archer, but since when he shoots, it will be obvious he is a very poor shot, the Friend tries to teach him a song which if recited well will be the necessary talent. The Groom cannot even remember the

293

simple song, so the Friend promises to go along, hide in the bushes, and prompt him. However, when the time comes, he, of course, cannot shoot, and even with vigorous prompting from the Friend, he can't get the song right. Finally the Friend gets disgusted, gives up and goes home. The Groom, left with no prompter and no memory, finally gives up hope of gaining a wife, apologizes and goes home.

YOBI KOE 呼声 (Tricked by a Rhythm) O 大

Shite	TARŌ KAJA
Ado	MASTER
Koado	JIRŌ KAJA

Tarō Kaja has been absent from work for some time without permission. The Master orders Jirō Kaja to go kill Tarō Kaja, but Jirō Kaja objects, and pleads for Tarō Kaja's life. The Master finally agrees that he shouldn't be killed, and sends Jirō Kaja to see if Tarō Kaja is home. Jirō Kaja finds Tarō Kaja at home and warns him of the Master's anger. Tarō Kaja thanks him, and says to send the Master to see him. When the Master arrives, Tarō Kaja pretends to be out. The Master knows this is a lie, and is somehow amused by it. He knows that Tarō Kaja has always been unable to resist a rhythm, so he asks again if Tarō Kaja is home, this time saying everything with a beat. Sure enough Tarō Kaja isn't able to resist, and answers back on the beat. The Master begins to enjoy this game and uses several different rhythms, till finally Tarō Kaja comes dancing out. The Master catches him and scolds him soundly.

YOKOZA 横座
(The Cow Named Yokoza)

Shite   COW KEEPER
Ado   FARMER
Koado   COW (YOKOZA)

A Farmer has just bought a new Cow, but since he doesn't know much about cows, he takes it to a Friend who is a Cow Keeper to have it appraised.

The Cow Keeper recently had a cow stolen and is on his way to ask the Farmer if he has seen it. They meet on the road. The Cow Keeper is surprised when he sees the Farmer leading his Cow and demands that he return it immediately. The Farmer objects that he has just paid good money for the Cow, but if the Cow Keeper can prove it is his Cow, he will let him have it.

The Cow Keeper begins by explaining that it was born when he was in the middle of a gambling session. He brought the

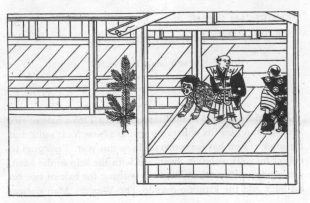

calf and put it beside him. His seat was the seat of honor, so the calf was is the second honored seat called *yokoza*. Everyone said that it was a lucky calf to have the second seat of honor so soon after being born, so the calf was named Yokoza. He goes on to explain that if he calls the Cow by name, it will answer.

The Farmer agrees to let the Cow Keeper call the Cow's name three times. If the Cow answers, the Cow Keeper can have it; if it doesn't answer, the Cow Keeper must become the Farmer's servant.

The Cow Keeper calls twice, and since he gets no answer, he recites a long chanted narrative (*katari*) which is full of double meanings threatening the Cow with its life if it doesn't answer when its name is called. At the end of this recitation, he calls the Cow's name once more, it answers, and the Cow Keeper starts off happily, his Cow regained. The Farmer runs out after him complaining, "At least give me back the new rope I put on the Cow!"

YONEICHI 米市
(A Rice Bale Mistaken for a Girl)

I O
和 大

Shite	TARŌ (MAN in Ōkura)
Ado	WEALTHY MAN
Tachishū	VILLAGERS

A Wealthy Man is in the habit of giving Tarō a bale of rice and a kimono for his wife every year as a New Year's gift, but for some reason has forgotten to do so this year. Tarō goes to collect his gifts, receives them, and with the help of the Man, gets ready to carry them home by putting the bale of rice on his back and the kimono over it. The Wealthy Man notices

296

that it looks as though Tarō is carrying a girl on his back, so he tells him that if anyone asks who it is to tell them it is Yoneichi (rice market) the daughter of Tōta Tawara (rice bale) and he is taking her to her home town.

On the way home he meets a group of Villagers, and sure enough, they ask him about his burden. He explains as his Wealthy Friend had told him to, and they unexpectedly respond that they want to have a drink with her.

Tarō explains that she is shy and refuses, they insist, he still refuses, and a fight ensues. During the fight one of the Villagers sneaks around behind Tarō, looks under the kimono and discovers the truth. They go off laughing at Tarō who goes on his way grumbling about the cruelty of young people and their insult to his precious gifts.

YOROI 鎧 (*See* Yoroi Haramaki)

YOROI HARAMAKI 鎧腹巻
(Armour on Paper)

Shite	TARŌ KAJA
Ado	MASTER
Koado	SHYSTER

The Master orders Tarō Kaja to go to the capital to buy a suit of armour, and says that it must include a helmet, cheek protectors, shin protectors, and a piece of equipment that is very frightening when you see it coming toward you.

Tarō Kaja reaches the capital and realizes he has never seen a suit of armour, and doesn't know where to buy one, so he

begins shouting that he wants to buy a suit of armour. A shyster hears him, discovers he knows nothing, and sells him a sheet of paper on which is written a poem which includes the words for armour and the necessary accessories, and for the frightening piece of equipment, a demon mask.

Tarō Kaja takes these things home, and when the Master asks to see the armour, he takes out the sheet of paper and reads the poem. When the Master asks for the frightening piece of equipment, he puts on the mask and pretends to be a demon. The Master realizes what has happened and scolds him soundly for his stupidity.

In the Ōkura script Tarō Kaja frightens the Master with the mask. When the Master realizes it is only Tarō Kaja, he grabs the mask, puts it on himself and chases Tarō Kaja off. The rest is the same as the Izumi script.

YUKI UCHI 雪打 (The Snow Fight)

Shite	OLD PRIEST
Ado	BOY
Koado	FARMER
Koado	WOMAN

A Boy begins sweeping the snow from his own yard to the yard next door. The Farmer comes out to sweep the snow from his own yard, and is very angry when he sees it piled high from the Boy's yard. The Farmer scolds the Boy, and tells him that the law states that everyone must keep their own snow in their own yard. The Boy responds that this is a much heavier snow than usual, so that the law doesn't apply, and if the Farmer doesn't like the snow in his yard, he can throw it into the next yard.

A Old Priest comes out to pray and look at the snow. The Farmer asks the Old Priest to settle the quarrel. The Old Priest agrees and sides with the Boy.

The Farmer gets even angrier because he knows the law is on his side. The Farmer and the Boy begin throwing snowballs at each other.

The Woman comes out to stop the fight, because the Boy is her and the Old Priest's son. When the Farmer hears this he says, 'What's this! The whole family of you ganging up on a law abiding citizen. I'll fix you!' And he chases them all off cursing.

YUMI YA 弓矢
(The Bow Maker and the Arrow Maker)

Shite	ARROW MAKER FROM HARIMA
Ado	BOW MAKER FROM IZUMI
Koado	TAX COLLECTOR

A Bow Maker from Izumi and an Arrow Maker from Harima meet on the road. They are both on their way to the capital to pay their annual taxes, so they decide to travel together.

They reach the capital, pay their taxes, and are ordered by the Tax Collector to tell the history of the bow and arrow. They agree to tell what they know about them, if he will allow them to recite together. The Tax Collector agrees and they tell their stories in a chanted narrative (*katari*) duet. The Tax Collector rewards them with *saké*, then orders them to sing and dance all the way home. They go off singing and dancing happily.

YUMI YA TARŌ 弓矢太郎
(Bow and Arrow Tarō)

Shite	TARŌ
Ado	HOST
Koado	TARŌ KAJA
Koado	GUESTS

A certain study group gathers for their regular meeting. Everyone has arrived except Tarō, so they begin gossiping and joking about him. Though Tarō is a well-known coward,

300

he is always dressed as a hunter, carries a bow and arrows, and brags about his brave deeds. They decide to spend the evening telling scary stories, and see how Tarō reacts.

Tarō finally arrives, apologizes, and explains that he has been out hunting. The Host begins the meeting by telling about a beautiful girl who was actually a fox in disguise, and would change back into a fox when it got dark and all the lights were put out. Everyone thoroughly enjoys this story and someone suggests that they put out the lights, and see if there are any foxes in the group. Tarō objects saying it is already too dark, and suggests that more lights be brought in.

The next story is about one of the men who went for a walk in a dark forest on a night of the full moon, and when he passed under the branches of a particularly huge pine tree, he looked up and saw the face of a demon, and before he could run away, a big hairy arm grabbed ahold of him.

At this point Tarō passes out, and when he comes to, explains that the story was so interesting that he simply dozed off. Everyone laughs at his cowardice, and he says that he has never been frightened in his whole life.

Since he claims to be so brave, the Host challenges him to take a fan and hang it on a certain pine tree in the nearby forest before dawn, and he will win a large sum of money. If he fails, he will become the Host's bond servant. Tarō agrees, takes the fan, and leaves.

The Host disguises himself as a demon, and goes to the pine tree to frighten Tarō. Tarō, also dressed as a demon, soon appears to hang up the fan, and when the two meet, they both pass out.

Tarō comes to first, and just as he is getting up to make a run for home, the rest of the group arrive with torches to see how things have turned out. Tarō quickly hides behind the tree.

They find the Host, take off his mask, and he tells them what has happened. They all begin to feel uncomfortable, when Tarō jumps out at them in his demon disguise. They all take off for home as fast as their legs will carry them, with Tarō close at their heels growling and shouting, "I'll catch you, and eat you all alive!"

YŪZEN 祐善 I O
(Yūzen, the Unskillful Umbrella Maker) 和 大

Shite	GHOST OF YŪZEN
Waki	TRAVELLING PRIEST
Ai	VILLAGER

A Travelling Priest who was originally an umbrella maker is caught in a sudden shower. He takes shelter in a hut along the road, and is wondering what it is, or whose it is, when an

old man appears and introduces himself as the Ghost of Yūzen, and disappears.

The Priest asks a passing Villager who Yūzen was. The Villager explains that Yūzen was an umbrella maker who was very poor at making umbrellas, and since his umbrellas were so poorly made, no one would buy them. He finally lost his mind and died. The Villager asks the Priest to pray for Yūzen's soul.

The Priest prays, and Yūzen appears, and tells the story of his life and death in a dance and song.

This Kyōgen is a Nōgakari, meaning it is constructed in the form of a Noh Drama, but handles Kyōgen-like materials.